Quiches
pies and tarts

The Confident Cooking Promise of Success

Welcome to the world of Confident Cooking,
where recipes are double-tested by our team
of home economists to achieve a high standard
of success—and delicious results every time.

bay books

C O N T E

Roasted Pumpkin and Spinach Quiche, page 11

Sweet Potato, Pumpkin and Coconut Lattice Pies, page 48

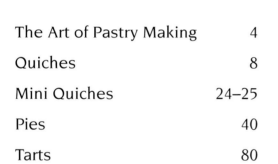

Italian Summer Tart, page 81

Moroccan Chicken Filo Pie, page 51

Fried Green Tomato Tart, page 106

Chicken and Watercress Strudel, page 68

The Publisher thanks the following for their assistance in the photography: The Bay Tree; Sirocco; East India Co.; HAG Imports, agents for Maxwell Williams; Ruby Star Traders.

All recipes are double-tested by our team of home economists. When we test our recipes, we rate them for ease of preparation. The following cookery ratings are on the recipes in this book, making them easy to use and understand.

A single Cooking with Confidence symbol indicates a recipe that is simple and generally quick to make —perfect for beginners.

Two symbols indicate the need for just a little more care and a little more time.

Three symbols indicate special dishes that need more investment in time, care and patience—but the results are worth it.

IMPORTANT
Those who might be at risk from the effects of salmonella food poisoning (the elderly, pregnant women, young children and those suffering from immune deficiency diseases) should consult their doctor with any concerns about eating raw eggs.

Asparagus and Artichoke Quiches, page 31

The Art of Pastry Making

Making pastry is often seen as time-consuming and difficult. Here we show you that pastry making is quick and easy once you know what you are doing.

Each country has its own pastry: the French have *pâte brisée*; the Greeks have filo; the Hungarians have strudel and the Chinese have won ton. There are many types of pastry of which the most basic, essential and easy to make are shortcrust and rich shortcrust pastry.

As with many things, once you have practised enough you'll soon get the feel for pastry making. It is simple to master, and with a few tips under your belt (such as handling the pastry as little as possible and being as lighthanded as you can) you'll be able to make pastry with no trouble.

Most of the recipes in this book use either the shortcrust or rich shortcrust pastry and have been made using a food processor. You can of course get superb results making your pastry by hand.

SHORTCRUST PASTRY

2 cups (250 g/8 oz) plain flour
125 g (4 oz) cold butter,
 chopped into small pieces
3–4 tablespoons cold water

1 Sift the flour into a bowl. Cut the butter into small pieces and add to the flour. Using your fingertips, quickly and lightly rub the butter into the flour until it resembles fine breadcrumbs.
2 Make a well in the centre of the flour mixture and add 2–3 tablespoons of water. Using a flat-bladed knife, mix until it binds together.
3 On a lightly floured surface, form the pastry into a ball. Cover thoroughly with plastic wrap and place in the refrigerator (to allow it to rest) for at least 20–30 minutes.

You can easily transform a basic shortcrust pastry into a rich shortcrust pastry by gradually adding a beaten egg yolk. Follow the recipe alongside, adding a beaten egg yolk to the flour with 2–3 tablespoons of water, as in Step 2. With a flat-bladed knife, mix until it binds together.

VARIATIONS ON SHORTCRUST PASTRY

You can change the taste and texture of your pastry by adding the following ingredients to your flour:
Sesame or poppy seed pastry: add 2 tablespoons of sesame or poppy seeds to the flour.
Nut pastry: add 3–4 tablespoons of ground nuts to the flour such as walnuts, almonds or pecans.
Herb pastry: add 2–3 tablespoons of your choice of chopped fresh herbs to the flour.
Mustard pastry: add 1–2 tablespoons of wholegrain mustard to the flour.

FOOD PROCESSOR PASTRY

The main advantage of using a food processor is its speed. As you don't touch the pastry often it also does not become too warm. Be careful not to overprocess the pastry or it will toughen. In order to control the amount of time you use to process the pastry, process in short bursts. Combine the ingredients for a maximum of 10 seconds at a time. You will know you have overprocessed the pastry if it forms into a ball in the processor. You want the pastry to just clump together. Then gather it into a ball by hand on a lightly floured surface.

Rub the butter into the flour lightly using your fingertips.

Make a well in the centre of the flour mixture and add the water.

Mix together quickly, using a flat-bladed knife.

Bring the dough together into a ball on a lightly floured surface.

FILO PASTRY

Filo pastry comprises very fine pastry sheets which can be bought in a roll either frozen or chilled. If it is frozen, allow it to thaw in the refrigerator for 24 hours. Most filo pastry recipes in this book use 5–6 sheets to give a firm base to your pie. To remove the sheets from the roll, unfold them so that they lie out flat and cover with baking paper. Then cover the baking paper with a damp tea towel. This prevents the sheets from drying out too quickly. Work with 1 sheet at a time, keeping the rest covered, and brush with either oil or melted butter.

Keep any unused pastry sheets well covered in foil. You can store the sheets in the refrigerator for up to 3 days. Do not refreeze any filo pastry once it has been opened and thawed. However, if unopened, the pastry can be stored in the freezer for up to 1 month.

READY-MADE PASTRY

Bought puff, butterpuff and vegetable oil puff and shortcrust pastries come as ready-rolled sheets. Standard puff and shortcrust pastry also come in a block. If you can't find butterpuff pastry, you can easily make your own; buy plain puff pastry and brush with melted butter.

Allow frozen block pastry to defrost for 2 hours before using. Ready-rolled sheets take 5–10 minutes to defrost at room temperature.

THE SECRETS OF PERFECT PASTRY: SEVEN STEPS TO SUCCESS

1 Air: Aerating the flour before mixing assists in keeping the finished pastry crisp and light. You can do this by either sifting the flour through a sieve or by pulsing it 7 or 8 times in a food processor.

2 Cool temperatures: Cool temperatures are vital. If the pastry is too soft and warm, it becomes sticky and unmanageable. If it is a hot day, chill the butter and water for as long as possible and keep chilling the pastry if it becomes difficult to work with. Also, if your hands are too hot, wash in very cold water and dry thoroughly. Use your fingertips to blend the butter into the flour as the palms of your hands are too warm.

3 Mixing: For a basic shortcrust pastry do not knead the dough. It should be just pressed together to form a ball. If it is kneaded, the dough becomes overworked causing the pastry to toughen. Therefore, handle the pastry quickly, lightly and as little as possible.

4 Liquid: Chill the water and sprinkle it over the flour mixture, 1 tablespoon at a time. The moisture content of flours varies from brand to brand so it is difficult to give the exact amount of water you should use. Cut the water through the flour with a flat-bladed knife, until the dough just comes together; don't stir. Form a ball using your hands. The dough should hold together

Lift the pastry over the tin and unroll or unfold gently.

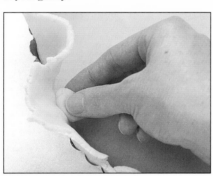
Use a small ball of excess dough to press down and into the seam of the tin.

Roll the rolling pin across the top of the tin, pressing down firmly.

without crumbling. If the dough is too wet and sticky, lightly sprinkle with a little flour and gather it into a ball on a well-floured surface; if it is too dry and cracks, sprinkle with a little more water.

5 Chilling and rolling: Allowing the pastry to rest makes it easier to roll and helps to prevent it from shrinking during cooking. Cover the ball with plastic wrap and refrigerate for at least 20–30 minutes before rolling. If the weather is hot, refrigerate for at least 30 minutes. Roll out the pastry on a lightly floured surface, using a rolling pin. The cooler the surface the better. A marble slab is perfect for this as it maintains a cool surface. However, a wood board, plastic pastry sheet or any flat surface are adequate.

6 Lining the tin: Place the rolling pin at one end of the pastry and lightly wrap it around the rolling pin. Place it over the tin or pie dish and unroll the pastry, taking care not to stretch it. Using a small ball of left-over dough, press the pastry onto the bottom and sides of the tin. Roll the rolling pin gently but firmly across the top of the tin to remove any excess pastry.

7 Resting: Once you have lined the tin according to the recipe you are following, chill the pastry again for at least 20–30 minutes before baking to allow it to relax. This reduces shrinkage during cooking.

BAKING BLIND

Baking blind is partially cooking the empty pastry case before the filling is added. This prevents the pastry from becoming soggy once you have added the filling.

1 After the pastry has rested in its tin, cover with baking paper. Fill with ceramic or baking beads. If you do not have these, uncooked rice or any dried beans are suitable.

2 Bake the pastry in a moderately hot 190°C (375°F/Gas 5) oven for the time specified in the recipe. Then remove the baking paper and beads before baking, uncovered, for a further 10 minutes. The pastry should be lightly golden. The cooled rice, beads or beans can be stored in a sealed jar and used over and over again.

Line the pastry with a sheet of baking paper and cover with baking beads.

Carefully lift the baking beads out of the pastry shell.

Another easy method for baking blind is to prick the base of the pastry case all over with a fork. This prevents the pastry rising and allows the trapped air to escape during baking. Bake for 20 minutes in a warm 170°C (325°F/Gas 3) oven. The pastry should be golden and crisp.

COVERING A PIE

You can use both puff and shortcrust pastry for making a lid to cover a pie.

1 On baking paper, roll out the dough 5 cm (2 inches) larger than the dish. To make a lid, cut the pastry 1 cm (1/2 inch) wider than the dish; then cut out a collar as wide as the rim of the pie dish. Set aside.

2 Place the pie funnel in the centre of the dish and place the cold filling around the funnel which supports the pastry and allows steam to escape.

3 Brush the rim of the dish with water and place the collar around the edge. You may need to join up several strips to cover the rim completely. Brush with water.

4 Wrap the pastry around the rolling pin and lift it over the top of the dish. Unwrap, then trim the edges with a sharp knife. Using the back of a knife, mark the rim of the pastry at intervals around the edges, to create ridges. This separates the edges of the pie when using puff pastry.

5 Using a sharp knife, cut a hole around the pie funnel and brush with some beaten egg yolk to glaze.

Using a sharp knife, cut around the edge of the dish and cut out a collar.

Using the back of a knife, mark around the edge of the pie to create ridges.

GLAZING

A glaze consists of a beaten egg yolk (sometimes mixed with water, milk or cream) which is brushed over the pastry lid before baking. This gives the pastry a golden, glossy finish.

FREEZING PASTRY

You can make your pastry in advance and freeze it until needed; it will keep for up to 3 months. When ready to use, allow enough time to thaw overnight in the refrigerator. It can also be stored in the refrigerator for up to 2 days if it is well covered.

GENERAL HINTS

Most of the recipes in this book use specific measurements for the baking tins. The cooking time for your quiche, pie or tart is dependent on the size of the tin. If you don't have any baking tins, it might be worthwile investing in baking tins of various standard sizes such as a round 20 cm (8 inch) or 25 cm (10 inch) quiche tin with a removeable base; or a 24 cm (91/2 inch) round or rectangular ovenproof pie dish. We sometimes use equipment that we don't expect every household to have. For example, if you don't have a lattice cutter or pastry wheel, you can use a lightly floured, sharp knife instead.

If you find that your pastry base is not cooking on the bottom, place a metal baking tray in the oven to heat as the oven warms up. When the oven is at the correct temperature, place your prepared tin or pie dish on the baking tray; you will find that the bottom of the pastry will cook much more quickly. Place the filling into the tin or pie dish while on the preheated tray.

The reason for adding a collar to your pie is to enable the pastry lid to stick to the pie dish without it lifting up while cooking.

To test whether your pie is thoroughly cooked through, insert a metal skewer into the centre of the pie. If the skewer is cold to touch, the pie needs to cook for a little longer in the oven.

DECORATING PIES

Traditionally, savoury pies were decorated to differentiate them at a glance from sweet pies when both were served at meals. Nowadays we use trimmings for mainly decorative effect.

Using any leftover pastry trimmings, you can finish off your pie with decorations. These are quick to do and transform the look of your pie. Once you have covered the pie, simply cut out the shapes you want, glaze the pie lid then lay the decorations on the pie lid and brush with a glaze. You can make many shapes or forms such as leaves or abstract patterns—or you can make a special, personalised pie with someone's initials or age.

If you don't want to make up your own designs, you can buy pastry cutters which come in many styles. Small biscuit cutters of various shapes are ideal for this. With a decorative cutter, cut shapes out of the centre of the pastry sheet. Using a rolling pin, carefully wrap the pastry around the pin, lay the pastry on top of the pie and unwrap. Then lightly glaze the pastry with some beaten egg yolk or water.

If you don't have decorative cutters, or want to make more complicated shapes, find an image in a book and trace around it to make a template. Transfer the image onto some firm card and cut out the shape.

Place the card onto the pastry and, using a lightly floured sharp knife, cut around your shape.

Shells, bells, cacti, hearts, leaves, coins or fish are easy to do. For the veins on the leaves or the scales on a fish, lightly score the dough with the tip of a knife.

The shape of a particular vegetable or fruit is especially effective if it is in the pie you are making. Try eggplants, onions, mushrooms, tomatoes, zucchini or carrots.

You can also pattern the pie by sprinkling 3–4 tablespoons of sesame or poppy seeds on the glazed lid before baking.

LATTICE TOP

With a little practice, making a lattice top is quite simple. Roll out the pastry to a circle on a sheet of baking paper. Using a lightly floured pastry cutter or sharp knife, cut sheets of pastry into long strips 1.5 cm (5/8 inch) wide. On another sheet of baking paper, lay half the strips vertically, 1 cm (1/2 inch) apart. Fold back alternate strips and weave a piece horizontally across the vertical strips. Repeat with the remaining strips. Refrigerate the strips until firm, then invert onto the pie and remove the baking paper. Press the edges together and trim any overhanging pastry using a sharp knife. Glaze with beaten egg and bake as directed in the recipe.

EDGES

On a double-crust pie it is important to seal the top and bottom layers of pastry so that the lid remains securely in place. Crimping the pastry seals the crust and decorates the edge. Crimping is done using your fingers, kitchen scissors, the back of a knife, an upturned teaspoon or the tines (prongs) of a fork. The easiest way to crimp the edges is to press them gently but firmly with the tines of a fork. Or, using your thumb and forefinger, pinch or crimp the edges together. For a scalloped effect, use an upturned teaspoon and press gently onto the pastry edges. You can also create a feathered effect with kitchen scissors; gently snip the edges of the pastry and they will rise up attractively during baking.

Pinch or crimp the edges of the pie using your thumb and forefinger.

Use a template to make a fish pattern and a straw for the holes.

Roll out the remaining pastry and cut into thin strips to make a lattice top.

Use the back of a teaspoon to make decorative patterns on the edges.

QUICHES

QUICHE LORRAINE

Preparation time: 35 minutes
  + 35 minutes refrigeration
Total cooking time: 1 hour 5 minutes
Serves 4–6

1¹/2 cups (185 g/6 oz) plain
  flour
90 g (3 oz) cold butter, chopped
1 egg yolk

Filling
20 g (³/4 oz) butter
1 onion, chopped
4 rashers bacon, cut into thin
  strips
2 tablespoons chopped chives
2 eggs
³/4 cup (185 ml/6 fl oz) cream
¹/4 cup (60 ml/2 fl oz) milk
100 g (3¹/2 oz) Swiss cheese,
  grated

1 Place the flour and butter in a food processor and combine for 15 seconds, or until crumbly. Add the egg yolk and 2–3 tablespoons of water. Process in short bursts until the mixture just comes together. Add a little extra water if needed. Turn the mixture out onto a floured surface and gather together into a ball. Cover with plastic wrap and refrigerate for at least 15 minutes.
2 Roll the pastry between two sheets of baking paper until it is large enough to fit and overlap a shallow loose-based round flan tin measuring 25 cm (10 inches) across the base. Lift the pastry into the tin and press it well into the sides. Trim off any excess pastry using a sharp knife or by rolling the rolling pin across the top of the tin. Place the pastry-lined flan tin in the refrigerator for 20 minutes. Preheat the oven to moderately hot 190°C (375°F/Gas 5).
3 Cover the pastry shell with baking paper, fill evenly with baking beads and bake for 15 minutes. Remove the paper and beads and bake for a further 10 minutes, or until the pastry has dried out. Reduce the oven to moderate 180°C (350°F/Gas 4).
4 To make the filling, heat the butter in a heavy-based pan. Add the onion and bacon and cook for 10 minutes, stirring frequently, until the onion is soft and the bacon is cooked. Stir through the chives and set aside to allow to cool.
5 Beat the eggs, cream and milk together in a jug. Season with freshly ground black pepper. Spread the onion and bacon mixture evenly over the base of the pastry shell. Pour the egg mixture over the onion and bacon and sprinkle with the cheese. Bake for 30 minutes, or until the filling has set and the top is golden.

NUTRITION PER SERVE (6)
Protein 15 g; Fat 40 g; Carbohydrate 25 g; Dietary Fibre 2 g; Cholesterol 210 mg; 2185 kJ (520 cal)

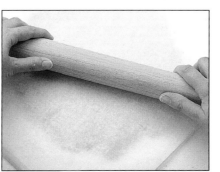

Roll out the pastry between two sheets of baking paper.

Pour the egg mixture over the onion and bacon in the base of the pastry shell.

OYSTER AND NUTMEG QUICHE

Preparation time: 20 minutes
 + 20 minutes refrigeration
Total cooking time: 1 hour
Serves 4

1 sheet ready-rolled shortcrust
    pastry
2 eggs
2 teaspoons plain flour
1/4 teaspoon fresh grated nutmeg
2 tablespoons cream
2 tablespoons milk

1/2 cup (65 g/2¹/4 oz) grated
    Gruyère cheese
1 dozen fresh oysters, shelled
20 g (³/4 oz) Parmesan, shaved

1 Use the pastry to line a shallow loose-based flan tin measuring 19 cm (7¹/2 inches) across the base. Press the pastry into the sides and trim off any excess using a sharp knife or by rolling the rolling pin across the top of the tin. Refrigerate for 20 minutes. Preheat the oven to moderate 180°C (350°F/Gas 4). Cover the pastry shell with baking paper and fill evenly with baking beads. Bake for 10 minutes.

Remove the paper and beads and bake for a further 5 minutes, or until the pastry is lightly golden. Cool on a wire rack.
2 Beat the eggs in a bowl then whisk in the flour, nutmeg, cream, milk and a pinch of salt. Stir in the cheese and pour over the base of the pastry shell.
3 Arrange the oysters on top of the quiche. Scatter the Parmesan over the top and bake for 40–45 minutes. Cool slightly before serving.

NUTRITION PER SERVE
Protein 15 g; Fat 25 g; Carbohydrate 15 g; Dietary Fibre 1 g; Cholesterol 150 mg; 1415 kJ (335 cal)

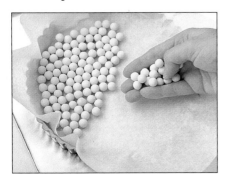

Cover the pastry shell with baking paper and fill evenly with baking beads.

Whisk the flour, nutmeg, cream, milk and salt into the beaten eggs.

Arrange the shelled oysters over the top of the quiche.

Roast the vegetables until lightly golden and cooked.

Line the flan tin with the six sheets of filo pastry.

Fold the sides of the filo pastry down and tuck them into the tin to form a crust.

ROASTED PUMPKIN AND SPINACH QUICHE

Preparation time: 20 minutes
Total cooking time: 1 hour 50 minutes
Serves 4–6

500 g (1 lb) butternut
    pumpkin
1 red onion, cut into small
    wedges
2 tablespoons olive oil
1 clove garlic, crushed
1 teaspoon salt
4 eggs
1/2 cup (125 ml/4 fl oz) cream
1/2 cup (125 ml/4 fl oz) milk
1 tablespoon parsley, chopped
1 tablespoon coriander,
    chopped
1 teaspoon wholegrain mustard
6 sheets filo pastry
50 g (1 3/4 oz) English spinach,
    blanched
1 tablespoon grated Parmesan

1 Preheat the oven to moderately hot 190°C (375°F/Gas 5). Slice the pumpkin into 1 cm (1/2 inch) pieces leaving the skin on. Place the pumpkin, onion, 1 tablespoon of the olive oil, garlic and salt in a baking dish. Roast for 1 hour, or until lightly golden and cooked.

2 Whisk together the eggs, cream, milk, herbs and mustard. Season with salt and pepper.

3 Grease a loose-based fluted flan tin or ovenproof dish measuring 22 cm (8 3/4 inches) across the base. Brush each sheet of filo pastry with oil and then line the flan tin with the six sheets. Fold the sides down, tucking them into the tin to form a crust.

4 Heat a baking tray in the oven for 10 minutes. Place the flan tin on the tray and arrange all the vegetables over the base. Pour the egg mixture over the vegetables and sprinkle with the Parmesan.

5 Bake for 35–40 minutes, or until the filling is golden brown and set.

Pour the egg and cream mixture over the vegetables in the lined flan tin.

NUTRITION PER SERVE (6)
Protein 10 g; Fat 20 g; Carbohydrate 15 g; Dietary Fibre 2 g; Cholesterol 155 mg; 1200 kJ (285 cal)

ZUCCHINI AND PROSCIUTTO QUICHE

Preparation time: 35 minutes
+ 20 minutes refrigeration
Total cooking time: 1 hour 15 minutes
Serves 6

2 sheets ready-rolled shortcrust
   pastry

Filling
olive oil, for cooking
150 g (5 oz) prosciutto
1 onion, chopped
4 zucchini, thinly sliced
4 eggs
2/3 cup (170 ml/5¹/2 fl oz) cream
1/4 cup (60 ml/2 fl oz) milk
1/4 cup (25 g/³/4 oz) grated
   Parmesan

1 Place the two sheets of pastry together, slightly overlapping. Roll out the pastry so that it is large enough to line a shallow loose-based fluted flan tin measuring 25 cm (10 inches) across the base. Lift the pastry into the tin, press into the sides and trim off any excess, using a sharp knife or by rolling a rolling pin across the top of the tin. Refrigerate for 20 minutes. Preheat the oven to moderately hot 200°C (400°F/Gas 6). Cover the pastry shell with baking paper and fill evenly with baking beads. Bake for 15 minutes. Remove the paper and beads and bake for a further 10 minutes, or until the pastry is lightly golden. Remove from the oven and cool on a wire rack.
2 To make the filling, heat about 2 tablespoons of olive oil in a frying pan. Cut the prosciutto into thin strips and sauté until it is crisp. Remove

from the pan with a slotted spoon and drain on paper towels. Sauté the onion until soft and remove from the pan. Sauté the zucchini—you may need to add a little more oil at this stage. When the zucchini is almost cooked season with salt and freshly ground black pepper. Remove from the heat.
3 Mix together the eggs, cream, milk and most of the Parmesan in a jug.

4 Lay the prosciutto, onion and zucchini over the pastry shell, then pour over the egg and milk mixture. Sprinkle over the remaining Parmesan. Bake for 35–40 minutes, until the filling has set and is golden.

NUTRITION PER SERVE
Protein 15 g; Fat 40 g; Carbohydrate 30 g; Dietary Fibre 2 g; Cholesterol 195 mg; 2215 kJ (525 cal)

Trim the excess pastry from the sides of the tin using a sharp knife.

Remove the sautéed prosciutto from the pan with a slotted spoon.

When almost cooked, season the zucchini with freshly ground black pepper.

Turn the pastry dough onto a floured surface and gather into a ball.

Prick all over the base of the pastry shell with a fork.

Scrunch up the salmon slices and arrange them around the edge of the quiche.

Process the cream cheese, eggs and mustard, then add the cream.

SMOKED SALMON AND CAPER QUICHE

Preparation time: 25 minutes
+ 40 minutes refrigeration
Total cooking time: 1 hour 10 minutes
Serves 6–8

1¹/2 cups (185 g/6 oz) plain flour
90 g (3 oz) cold butter, chopped
2 teaspoons cracked black peppercorns
1 egg yolk

Filling
1 small leek, chopped
¹/2 teaspoon sugar
8 slices smoked salmon
¹/3 cup (50 g/1³/4 oz) frozen peas
2 tablespoons capers, chopped
75 g (2¹/2 oz) cream cheese
2 eggs
2 teaspoons Dijon mustard
³/4 cup (185 ml/6 fl oz) cream

1 Process the flour and butter for 15 seconds until crumbly. Add the peppercorns, egg yolk and 2 table-spoons of water. Process in short bursts until the mixture comes together. Turn onto a floured surface and gather into a ball. Cover with plastic wrap and chill for 30 minutes. Preheat the oven to moderately hot 200°C (400°F/Gas 6). Grease a deep loose-based fluted flan tin measuring 17 cm (6³/4 inches) across the base.

2 Lay the pastry in the tin, place on a baking tray and chill for 10 minutes. Prick the base and bake for 12 minutes.

3 To make the filling, cook the leek and sugar in a little oil over low heat for 15 minutes. Cool, then spoon into the pastry. Scrunch up the salmon slices and lay around the edge. Place the peas and capers in the centre.

4 Process the cream cheese, eggs and mustard until smooth. Add the cream and pour into the pastry shell. Bake for 40 minutes, or until set.

NUTRITION PER SERVE (8)
Protein 10 g; Fat 25 g; Carbohydrate 20 g; Dietary Fibre 2 g; Cholesterol 150 mg; 1485 kJ (355 cal)

MUSHROOM QUICHE WITH PARSLEY PASTRY

Preparation time: 30 minutes
  + 50 minutes refrigeration
Total cooking time: 1 hour
Serves 4–6

1¼ cups (155 g/5 oz) plain flour
¼ cup (15 g/½ oz) chopped
   parsley
90 g (3 oz) cold butter, chopped
1 egg yolk

Mushroom Filling
30 g (1 oz) butter
1 red onion, chopped
175 g (6 oz) button
   mushrooms, sliced
1 teaspoon lemon juice
⅓ cup (20 g/¾ oz) chopped
   parsley
⅓ cup (20 g/¾ oz) chopped
   chives
1 egg, lightly beaten
⅓ cup (80 ml/2¾ oz) cream

1 Process the flour, parsley and butter for 15 seconds, or until crumbly. Add the egg yolk and 2 tablespoons of water. Process in short bursts until the mixture comes together. Add a little extra water if needed. Turn out onto a floured surface and gather into a ball. Cover with plastic wrap and refrigerate for at least 30 minutes.
2 Roll out the pastry between 2 sheets of baking paper until big enough to fit a loose-based flan tin measuring 35 x 10 cm (14 x 4 inches) across the base. Lift the pastry over the rolling pin and fit it into the tin. Trim off any excess pastry by rolling the rolling pin across the top of the

tin. Refrigerate for 20 minutes. Preheat the oven to moderately hot 190°C (375°F/Gas 5). Cover the pastry with baking paper and fill evenly with baking beads. Bake for 15 minutes. Remove the paper and beads and bake for a further 10 minutes, or until the pastry has dried out. Reduce the oven to moderate 180°C (350°F/Gas 4).
3 To make the mushroom filling, melt the butter in a pan and cook the onion for 2–3 minutes until soft. Add

the mushrooms and cook, stirring, for 2–3 minutes until soft. Stir in the lemon juice and herbs. Mix the egg and cream in a small jug and season.
4 Spread the mushroom mixture into the pastry shell and pour over the combined egg and cream. Bake for 25–30 minutes, or until set.

NUTRITION PER SERVE (6)
Protein 6 g; Fat 25 g; Carbohydrate 20 g; Dietary Fibre 2 g; Cholesterol 130 mg; 1350 kJ (320 cal)

Place the flour and parsley in a food processor and add the butter.

Use the rolling pin to lift the pastry into the flan tin.

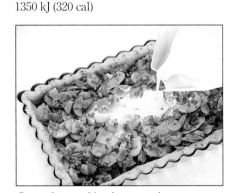

Pour the combined egg and cream over the mushroom filling.

PRAWN, CRAB AND CHEESE QUICHES

Preparation time: 45 minutes
  + 30 minutes refrigeration
Total cooking time: 40 minutes
Serves 4

2 cups (250 g/8 oz) plain flour
125 g (4 oz) cold butter,
  chopped
2 egg yolks

Crab and Cheese Filling
170 g (5¹/2 oz) can crab meat,
  drained and squeezed dry
4 spring onions, chopped
2 eggs, lightly beaten
1 cup (250 ml/8 fl oz) cream
1 cup (125 g/4 oz) finely grated
  Cheddar
2 tablespoons chopped dill
1 teaspoon grated lemon rind
200 g (6¹/2 oz) small prawns,
  cooked and peeled

1 Process the flour and butter for 15 seconds, or until crumbly. Add the egg yolks and 3–4 tablespoons of water. Process in short bursts until the mixture comes together. Add a little extra water if needed. Turn out onto a floured surface and gather into a ball. Cover the pastry with plastic wrap and refrigerate for at least 15 minutes.
2 Grease eight 3 cm (1¹/4 inch) deep loose-based flan tins, measuring 8 cm (3 inches) across the base. Divide the pastry into 8 equal pieces and roll out so they are large enough to fit and overlap the tins. Fit the pastry into the tins and trim off any excess using a sharp knife. Cover and refrigerate for 15 minutes. Preheat the oven to

moderately hot 190°C (375°F/Gas 5). Cover the pastry shells with baking paper and fill evenly with baking beads. Bake for 10 minutes. Remove the paper and beads and bake for a further 10 minutes.
3 To make the filling, place the crab meat, spring onions, beaten eggs, cream, cheese, chopped dill and lemon rind in a bowl. Season with freshly ground black pepper. Divide the prawns between the pastry shells. The crab mixture will be quite thick, so use a fork to help spread it over the prawns. Bake for 15–20 minutes, or until the filling is golden brown.

NUTRITION PER SERVE
Protein 15 g; Fat 35 g; Carbohydrate 25 g; Dietary Fibre 1 g; Cholesterol 255 mg; 1990 kJ (475 cal)

Squeeze small amounts of crab meat with your hand to get rid of excess moisture.

Roll out the pastry so that it is large enough to fit the prepared tins.

Use a fork to help you spread the crab mixture into the pastry shells.

POTATO, LEEK AND SPINACH QUICHE

Preparation time: 1 hour
  + 50 minutes refrigeration
Total cooking time: 2 hours
Serves 6–8

2 cups (250 g/8 oz) plain flour
125 g (4 oz) cold butter,
     chopped

Filling
3 medium potatoes
30 g (1 oz) butter
2 tablespoons oil
2 cloves garlic, crushed
2 leeks, sliced
500 g (1 lb) English spinach,
     trimmed
1 cup (125 g/4 oz) grated
     Cheddar
4 eggs
1/2 cup (125 ml/4 fl oz) cream
1/2 cup (125 ml/4 fl oz) milk

1 Place the flour in a food processor, add the butter and process for about 15 seconds until the mixture is crumbly. Add 2–3 tablespoons of water and process in short bursts until the mixture just comes together when you squeeze a little between your fingers. Add a little extra water if necessary. Turn out onto a floured surface and quickly bring the mixture together into a ball. Cover the pastry with plastic wrap and refrigerate for at least 30 minutes. Roll the pastry out between 2 sheets of baking paper until it is large enough to line a deep loose-based fluted flan tin measuring 21 cm (81/2 inches) across the base. Place on a baking tray and refrigerate for 20 minutes.

2 Peel and thinly slice the potatoes. Melt the butter and oil together in a frying pan; add the garlic and sliced potatoes. Gently turn the potatoes until they are coated, then cover and cook for 5 minutes over low heat. Remove the potatoes with a slotted spoon, drain on paper towels and set aside. Add the leeks to the pan and cook until they are softened, then remove from the heat. Place the spinach in a large saucepan, cover and cook for 2 minutes, or until it has just wilted. Cool the spinach and squeeze out any excess water, then spread the leaves out on a paper towel or a tea towel to allow to dry.
3 Preheat the oven to moderate 180°C (350°F/Gas 4). Cover the pastry shell with baking paper and fill evenly with baking beads. Bake for 15 minutes. Remove the paper and beads and bake for a further 15 minutes.
4 Spread half the cheese over the bottom of the pastry base, top with half the potatoes, half the spinach and half the leeks. Repeat these layers again. In a large jug mix together the eggs, cream and milk and pour over the layered mixture. Bake for 1 hour 20 minutes, or until the filling is firm. Serve warm or cold.

NUTRITION PER SERVE (8)
Protein 15 g; Fat 35 g; Carbohydrate 35 g; Dietary Fibre 5 g; Cholesterol 180 mg; 2150 kJ (510 cal)

COOK'S FILE

Note: Spinach can be kept in a plastic bag and stored for up to 3 days in the refrigerator. It is usually very gritty, so wash thoroughly in a few changes of water. Squeeze and dry well on paper towels or a tea towel so that the excess water does not make the filling too moist.

Squeeze a little of the pastry with your fingers, it should stick together.

Roll the pastry out between 2 sheets of baking paper.

Remove the potatoes with a slotted spoon and drain on paper towels.

Cook the spinach for 2 minutes, or until it has just wilted.

Squeeze out the excess water from the cooled spinach.

Layer half of the cheese, potato, spinach and leek over the pastry base.

TOMATO AND BACON QUICHE

Preparation time: 45 minutes
+ 1 hour refrigeration
Total cooking time: 1 hour 10 minutes
Serves 6

1^{1}/2 cups (185 g/6 oz) plain
    flour, sifted
pinch of cayenne pepper
pinch of mustard powder
125 g (4 oz) cold butter,
    chopped
1/3 cup (40 g/1^{1}/4 oz) grated
    Cheddar
1 egg yolk

Filling
25 g (3/4 oz) butter
100 g (3^{1}/2 oz) bacon, rind and
    excess fat removed, chopped
1 small onion, finely sliced
3 eggs
3/4 cup (185 ml/6 fl oz) cream
1/2 teaspoon salt
2 tomatoes, peeled, seeded and
    chopped into chunks
3/4 cup (90 g/3 oz) grated mature
    Cheddar

1 Process the flour, pepper, mustard and butter until crumbly. Add the cheese and egg yolk and process in short bursts until the mixture comes together. Add 1–2 tablespoons of water if needed. Turn out onto a floured surface and gather into a ball. Cover with plastic wrap and refrigerate for 30 minutes. Grease a 3.5 cm (1^{1}/2 inch) deep loose-based flan tin measuring 22 cm (8^{3}/4 inches) across the base.
2 To make the filling, melt the butter in a frying pan and cook the bacon for a few minutes over medium heat until golden. Add the onion and cook until soft. Remove from the heat. Lightly beat the eggs, cream and salt in a bowl. Add the bacon and onion, then fold in the tomato and Cheddar.
3 Roll out the pastry on a floured surface and fit into the tin. Place in the refrigerator for 30 minutes. Preheat the oven to moderate 180°C (350°F/Gas 4). Cover the pastry shell with baking paper and fill with baking beads. Bake for 10 minutes. Remove the paper and beads and bake for a further 10 minutes.
4 Pour the filling into the pastry shell and bake for 35 minutes, or until golden.

NUTRITION PER SERVE
Protein 15 g; Fat 45 g; Carbohydrate 25 g; Dietary Fibre 2 g; Cholesterol 255 mg; 2405 kJ (570 cal)

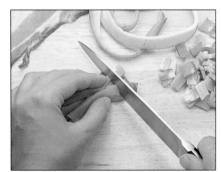

Remove the rind and excess fat from the bacon and chop the meat.

Add the onion to the bacon and cook until soft.

Fold the tomato chunks and Cheddar into the egg and cream mixture.

CARAMELISED ONION QUICHE

Preparation time: 45 minutes
+ 20 minutes refrigeration
Total cooking time: 1 hour 45 minutes
Serves 6

1¹/₂ cups (185 g/6 oz) plain flour
125 g (4 oz) cold butter, chopped
1 egg yolk

Filling
800 g (1 lb 10 oz) onions, thinly
    sliced
75 g (2¹/₂ oz) butter
1 tablespoon soft brown sugar
³/₄ cup (185 ml/6 fl oz) sour
    cream
2 eggs
40 g (1¹/₄ oz) prosciutto, cut
    into strips
40 g (1¹/₄ oz) grated mature
    Cheddar
2 teaspoons thyme leaves

1 Process the flour and butter and
process until crumbly. Add the egg
yolk and 1–2 tablespoons of water.
Process in short bursts until the
mixture comes together. Add extra
water if needed. Turn out and gather
into a ball. Cover with plastic wrap
and chill for 20 minutes.
2 Blanch the onion in boiling water
for 2 minutes, then drain. Melt the
butter in a pan and cook the onion
over low heat for 25 minutes, or until
soft. Stir in the brown sugar and cook
for a further 15 minutes, stirring
occasionally to prevent burning.
Preheat the oven to moderately
hot 200°C (400°F/Gas 6). Grease a
loose-based flan tin measuring
22.5 cm (8³/₄ inches) across the base.

3 Roll out the pastry until large
enough to fit the flan tin. Fit the
pastry into the tin, trimming off any
excess using a sharp knife. Cover with
baking paper and fill evenly with
baking beads. Bake for 15 minutes.
Remove the paper and beads and
bake for 5 minutes. Cool slightly.
4 Lightly beat the sour cream and
eggs together. Add the prosciutto,

cheese and thyme leaves. Season with
salt and pepper. Stir in the onion. Fill
the pastry shell with the onion
mixture. Bake for 40 minutes, or until
set. If the pastry starts to overbrown,
cover with a piece of foil.

NUTRITION PER SERVE
Protein 10 g; Fat 45 g; Carbohydrate 30 g;
Dietary Fibre 3 g; Cholesterol 230 mg;
2450 kJ (585 cal)

*Add the egg yolk to the processed flour
and butter.*

*Blanch the onion in a large saucepan
filled with boiling water.*

*Stir the soft brown sugar through the
softened onion.*

ARTICHOKE AND PROVOLONE QUICHES

Preparation time: 40 minutes
  + 30 minutes refrigeration
Total cooking time: 35 minutes
Serves 6

2 cups (250 g/8 oz) plain flour
125 g (4 oz) cold butter, chopped
1 egg yolk

Filling
1 small eggplant, sliced
6 eggs, lightly beaten
3 teaspoons wholegrain mustard
150 g (5 oz) provolone cheese, grated
200 g (6¹/₂ oz) marinated artichokes, sliced
125 g (4 oz) semi-dried tomatoes

1 Process the flour and butter in a processor for about 15 seconds until crumbly. Add the egg yolk and 3 tablespoons of water. Process in short bursts until the mixture comes together. Add a little extra water if needed. Turn out onto a floured surface and gather into a ball. Cover with plastic wrap and refrigerate for at least 30 minutes.

2 Preheat the oven to moderately hot 190°C (375°F/Gas 5) and grease six 11 cm (4¹/₂ inch) oval pie tins.
3 To make the filling, brush the sliced eggplant with olive oil and place under a grill until golden. Combine the eggs, mustard and cheese in a jug.
4 Roll out the pastry and line the tins. Trim the excess pastry and decorate the edges. Place one eggplant slice, the artichokes and tomatoes in the tins, pour the egg mixture over and bake for 25 minutes, or until golden.

NUTRITION PER QUICHE
Protein 20 g; Fat 30 g; Carbohydrate 35 g; Dietary Fibre 4 g; Cholesterol 290 mg; 2025 kJ (480 cal)

Gather the pastry into a ball and cover with plastic wrap.

Brush each slice of eggplant with a little olive oil.

Place one slice of eggplant in the bottom of each lined pie tin.

Fit the pastry into the flan tin, pressing it well into the sides.

Remove the baking paper and rice from the pastry shell.

Sauté the raw seafood in the melted butter until just cooked.

Sprinkle the grated Cheddar over the top of the seafood in the pastry shell.

SEAFOOD QUICHE

Preparation time: 20 minutes
  + 20 minutes refrigeration
Total cooking time: 1 hour
Serves 4–6

2 sheets ready-rolled shortcrust
  pastry

Filling
30 g (1 oz) butter
300 g (10 oz) mixed raw
  seafood (prawns, scallops,
  crab meat)
3/4 cup (90 g/3 oz) grated
  Cheddar
3 eggs
1 tablespoon plain flour
1/4 teaspoon salt
1/2 teaspoon black pepper
1/2 cup (125 ml/4 fl oz) cream
1/2 cup (125 ml/4 fl oz) milk
1 small fennel, finely sliced
1 tablespoon grated Parmesan

1 Place the 2 sheets of pastry slightly overlapping and roll out until large enough to fit a loose-based flan tin measuring 22 cm (8 3/4 inches) across the base. Lift the pastry into the tin and trim off any excess using a sharp knife. Refrigerate for 20 minutes. Preheat the oven to moderately hot 190°C (375°F/Gas 5). Cover the pastry shell with baking paper, fill evenly with rice and bake for 15 minutes. Remove the paper and rice and bake for 10 minutes, or until lightly golden. Cool on a wire rack.
2 Heat the butter in a pan and sauté the seafood for 2–3 minutes, or until cooked. Allow to cool, then arrange over the base of the pastry shell. Sprinkle with the Cheddar.
3 Beat the eggs in a small jug and whisk in the flour, salt, pepper, cream and milk. Pour the egg mixture over the quiche filling. Sprinkle the fennel and Parmesan over the top.
4 Bake for 30–35 minutes. Cool slightly before serving.

NUTRITION PER SERVE (6)
Protein 20 g; Fat 35 g; Carbohydrate 30 g; Dietary Fibre 1 g; Cholesterol 220 mg; 2190 kJ (520 cal)

GREEN PEPPERCORN AND GRUYERE QUICHES

Preparation time: 25 minutes
+ 15 minutes refrigeration
Total cooking time: 35 minutes
Makes 4

**2 sheets frozen ready-rolled
puff pastry, thawed**

Filling
**100 g (3½ oz) Gruyère cheese,
diced
½ small stick celery, finely
chopped
1 teaspoon chopped thyme
2 teaspoons green peppercorns,
chopped
1 egg, lightly beaten
¼ cup (60 ml/2 fl oz) cream
1 tablespoon rosemary**

1 Lightly grease 4 deep loose-based flan tins measuring 8 cm (3 inches) across the base. Cut two 14 cm (5½ inch) rounds from each sheet of pastry. Lift the pastry into the tins and press it well into the sides. Trim the excess pastry using a sharp knife or by rolling the rolling pin across the top of the tin. Prick the bases a few times with a fork. Refrigerate for at least 15 minutes.

2 Preheat the oven to hot 220°C (425°F/Gas 7). Bake the pastry shells for about 12 minutes, or until they are browned and puffed. Remove from the oven and, as the pastry is cooling, gently press down the bases if they have puffed too high—this will make room for the filling.

3 To make the filling, mix together the cheese, celery, thyme and peppercorns in a small bowl. Spoon the mixture into the pastry cases, then pour over the combined egg and cream. Sprinkle the tops of the quiches with the rosemary. Bake for 20 minutes, or until the filling is puffed and set.

NUTRITION PER QUICHE
Protein 15 g; Fat 35 g; Carbohydrate 30 g; Dietary Fibre 1 g; Cholesterol 115 mg; 2045 kJ (485 cal)

COOK'S FILE

Note: If it is available, use butterpuff pastry for this recipe.

Chop the Gruyère cheese, celery and thyme.

Use a bowl or plate as a guide to help you cut out the pastry.

Gently press down the bases of the pastry shells if they have puffed up too high.

Sprinkle the tops of the quiches with rosemary.

SPICY SWEET POTATO QUICHE

Preparation time: 30 minutes
+ 20 minutes refrigeration
Total cooking time: 1 hour 35 minutes
Serves 6

2 cups (250 g/8 oz) plain flour
125 g (4 oz) cold butter,
    chopped
1 egg yolk

Filling
30 g (1 oz) butter
1 onion, sliced
1 clove garlic, crushed
2 teaspoons black mustard seeds
2 teaspoons ground cumin
1 teaspoon soft brown sugar
450 g (14 oz) orange sweet
    potato, chopped
2 eggs, lightly beaten
1/4 cup (60 ml/2 fl oz) milk
1/4 cup (60 ml/2 fl oz) cream
2 tablespoons chopped parsley
2 tablespoons chopped chives

1 Process the flour and butter for about 15 seconds until crumbly. Add the egg yolk and 2–3 tablespoons of water. Process in short bursts until the mixture comes together. Add a little extra water if needed. Turn out onto a floured surface and gather into a ball. Roll the pastry between 2 sheets of baking paper until large enough to line a shallow loose-based fluted flan tin measuring 22 cm (8¾ inches) wide. Fit the pastry into the tin and trim the edges. Refrigerate for 20 minutes.
2 Heat the butter in a large pan and cook the onion and garlic for 5 minutes, or until golden. Add the mustard seeds, cumin and brown sugar and stir for 1 minute. Then add the sweet potato and cook for 10 minutes over low heat until it has softened slightly. Stir gently, or the sweet potato will break up.
3 Preheat the oven to moderate 180°C (350°F/Gas 4). Cover the pastry shell with baking paper and fill evenly with baking beads. Bake for 15 minutes, then remove the paper and beads and bake for a further 15 minutes.
4 Put the sweet potato mixture into the pastry, then add the combined eggs, milk, cream and herbs. Bake for 50 minutes, or until set.

NUTRITION PER SERVE
Protein 10 g; Fat 30 g; Carbohydrate 45 g; Dietary Fibre 4 g; Cholesterol 140 mg; 2015 kJ (480 cal)

Peel the sweet potato and cut into bite-sized chunks.

Add the mustard seeds, cumin and brown sugar to the onion and garlic.

Pour the combined eggs, milk, cream and herbs over the sweet potato mixture.

Mini Quiches

SMOKED SALMON AND DILL QUICHES

Roll 2 sheets of ready-rolled shortcrust pastry into 27 cm (10¾ inch) squares. Using a 7 cm (2¾ inch) plain or fluted cutter, cut 12 rounds from each sheet. Line 6 cm (2½ inch) patty tins with the pastry, cover and refrigerate for 10–15 minutes. Chop 100 g (3½ oz) smoked salmon and set aside one quarter. Mix the remaining salmon with 125 g (4 oz) light cream cheese, 2 lightly beaten eggs, 2 tablespoons mayonnaise, 1 tablespoon each of chopped chives and dill and 1 teaspoon of grated lemon rind. Fill the pastry shells with the salmon mixture. Bake in a preheated moderately hot 190°C (375°F/Gas 5) oven for 15–20 minutes, or until golden. Divide the remaining salmon over the top and garnish with dill. Makes 24.

NUTRITION PER QUICHE
Protein 3 g; Fat 6 g; Carbohydrate 7 g; Dietary Fibre 0 g; Cholesterol 25 mg; 380 kJ (90 cal)

CORN AND SEMI-DRIED TOMATO QUICHES

Roll 2 sheets of ready-rolled puff pastry into 27 cm (10¾ inch) squares. Using a 7 cm (2¾ inch) plain cutter, cut 12 rounds from each. Use the rounds to line 6 cm (2½ inch) diameter patty tins, cover and refrigerate for 10–15 minutes. Cut 12 semi-dried tomatoes in half and set aside. Cook 2 chopped rashers of bacon in 1 teaspoon of butter then place in a bowl with 2 lightly beaten eggs, ½ cup (125 ml/4 fl oz) sour cream, 310 g (10 oz) can creamed corn and 1 tablespoon chopped parsley. Fill each pastry shell with the corn mixture and top with a tomato half. Bake in a preheated moderately hot 190°C (375°F/Gas 5) oven for 15–20 minutes, or until puffed and golden. Makes 24.

NUTRITION PER QUICHE
Protein 3 g; Fat 6 g; Carbohydrate 8 g; Dietary Fibre 1 g; Cholesterol 25 mg; 420 kJ (100 cal)

CRAB AND SPRING ONION QUICHES

Butter and stack 6 sheets of filo pastry. Using an 8 cm (3 inch) plain cutter, cut 15 rounds. Place the pastry in 6 cm (2½ inch) diameter patty tins. Drain two 170 g (5½ oz) cans crab meat. Squeeze the meat dry with your hands. Cook 4 chopped spring onions in 1 teaspoon of butter until softened. Mix together the crab meat, spring onions, 2 beaten eggs, ¾ cup (185 ml/6 fl oz) cream, 1 tablespoon plain flour and 60 g (2 oz) shredded Gruyère cheese. Fill each pastry case with the crab filling and sprinkle with 30 g (1 oz) Gruyère cheese and place a sprig of thyme over the top. Bake in a preheated moderate 180°C (350°F/Gas 4) oven for 18–20 minutes, or until puffed and golden. Makes 15.

NUTRITION PER QUICHE
Protein 5 g; Fat 8 g; Carbohydrate 4 g; Dietary Fibre 0 g; Cholesterol 60 mg; 450 kJ (105 cal)

Mini quiches, from left: Smoked Salmon and Dill; Corn and Semi-dried Tomato; Crab and Spring Onion; Zucchini and Parmesan Boats; Mushroom Duxelle; Spinach and Prosciutto Brioche

ZUCCHINI AND PARMESAN BOATS

Roll 3 sheets of ready-rolled shortcrust pastry into 27 cm (11 inch) squares. Cut each sheet into 6 rectangles and use to line eighteen 12 x 5.5 cm (5 x 2 inch), 2 cm (3/4 inch) deep, greased fluted pastry boats. Refrigerate for 10–15 minutes. Cook 1 finely chopped small red onion and 1–2 crushed cloves garlic in 30 g (1 oz) butter until soft. Cool, then stir through 2 beaten eggs, 1/2 cup (125 ml/4 fl oz) sour cream, 1/3 cup (30 g/1 oz) shredded Parmesan, 1 thinly sliced small zucchini and black pepper, to taste. Spoon into the pastry boats and arrange a few extra slices of zucchini over the top. Bake at moderately hot 190°C (375°F/Gas 5) for 15 minutes, or until puffed and golden. Makes 18.

NUTRITION PER QUICHE
Protein 4 g; Fat 15 g; Carbohydrate 15 g; Dietary Fibre 1 g; Cholesterol 45 mg; 755 kJ (180 cal)

MUSHROOM DUXELLE QUICHES

Cook 300 g (10 oz) finely chopped button mushrooms and 4 chopped spring onions in a little butter for 4–5 minutes, or until soft and dry. Add 1 tablespoon chopped parsley. Cool. Add 2 beaten eggs and 2/3 cup (170 ml/5 1/2 fl oz) cream and season. Take 2 sheets of ready-rolled shortcrust pastry and, using a 6 cm (2 1/2 inch) fluted cutter, cut 12 circles from each sheet and use to line 6 cm (2 1/2 inch) patty tins. Cover and chill. Spoon in the filling and decorate with a slice of mushroom. Bake in a moderately hot 190°C (375°F/Gas 5) oven for 15 minutes, or until puffed and golden. Makes 24.

NUTRITION PER QUICHE
Protein 2 g; Fat 9 g; Carbohydrate 7 g; Dietary Fibre 1 g; Cholesterol 35 mg; 480 kJ (115 cal)

SPINACH AND PROSCIUTTO BRIOCHE QUICHES

Roll 4 sheets of ready-rolled shortcrust pastry into 27 cm (11 inch) squares, then cut each sheet into quarters and use to line sixteen 8 cm (3 inch) diameter 3 cm (1 1/4 inch) deep mini brioche tins. Cover and refrigerate for 10–15 minutes. Finely chop 1 small red onion, thinly slice 4 slices of prosciutto and cook for 2–3 minutes in a little butter with 2 crushed cloves of garlic. Stir in 1 cup (200 g/6 1/2 oz) wilted chopped English spinach, 1 cup (250 g/8 oz) ricotta cheese, 3 lightly beaten eggs, 1/2 cup (125 ml/4 fl oz) cream, 1/2 teaspoon nutmeg and season to taste. Spoon into the pastry cases and bake in a moderately hot 200°C (400°F/Gas 6) oven for 20 minutes, or until crisp and golden. Makes 16.

NUTRITION PER QUICHE
Protein 7 g; Fat 20 g; Carbohydrate 20 g; Dietary Fibre 1 g; Cholesterol 75 mg; 1160 kJ (275 cal)

FRESH SALMON AND DILL QUICHE

Preparation time: 35 minutes
  + 30 minutes refrigeration
Total cooking time: 55 minutes
Serves 4–6

1¹/₂ cups (185 g/6 oz) plain flour
125 g (4 oz) cold butter,
    chopped
1 teaspoon icing sugar

Filling
2 eggs
1 egg yolk
1 cup (250 ml/8 fl oz) cream
1 teaspoon finely grated lemon
    rind
2 tablespoons finely chopped
    spring onion
500 g (1 lb) fresh salmon fillet,
    bones and skin removed and
    cut into bite-sized chunks
1 tablespoon chopped dill

1 Process the flour, butter and icing sugar for about 15 seconds until crumbly. Add 1–2 tablespoons of water. Process in short bursts until the mixture just comes together. Add a little extra water if needed. Turn out onto a floured surface and gather into a ball. Cover the pastry with plastic wrap and refrigerate for 15 minutes.
2 Roll the pastry between 2 sheets of baking paper until it is large enough to fit a loose-based flan tin measuring 22 cm (8³/₄ inches) across the base. Fit the pastry into the tin and trim off any excess using a sharp knife. Place the lined flan tin in the refrigerator for 15 minutes. Preheat the oven to moderate 180°C (350°F/Gas 4).
3 To make the filling, lightly beat the eggs and egg yolk until combined. Add the cream, lemon rind and spring onion and season with salt and freshly ground black pepper. Cover and set aside.
4 Prick the base of the pastry with a fork. Cover with baking paper and fill evenly with baking beads or rice. Bake for 15 minutes, or until lightly golden. Remove the paper and beads or rice and arrange the salmon chunks over the base. Scatter the dill over the salmon and then pour over the egg mixture. Bake for 40 minutes, or until the salmon is cooked and the filling has set. Serve warm or cool.

NUTRITION PER SERVE (6)
Protein 25 g; Fat 45 g; Carbohydrate 25 g; Dietary Fibre 1 g; Cholesterol 255 mg; 2535 kJ (605 cal)

Cut the boned and skinned salmon fillet into bite-sized chunks.

Cover the pastry shell with baking paper and fill evenly with rice.

Scatter the chopped dill over the salmon in the pastry case.

BLUE CHEESE AND PARSNIP QUICHE

Preparation time: 45 minutes
 + 25 minutes refrigeration
Total cooking time: 1 hour 10 minutes
Serves 4–6

1 cup (125 g/4 oz) plain flour
1 cup (150 g/5 oz) wholemeal
   plain flour
100 g (3¼ oz) cold butter,
   chopped
1 egg yolk

Filling
1 tablespoon oil
1 onion, chopped
2 carrots, cut into small cubes
2 parsnips, cut into small cubes
2 teaspoons cumin seeds
2 tablespoons chopped
   coriander
200 g (6½ oz) mild blue cheese
2 eggs, lightly beaten
⅔ cup (185 ml/6 fl oz) cream

1 Process the flours and butter until crumbly. Add the egg yolk and 3 tablespoons of water. Process in short bursts until the mixture comes together. Add more water if needed. Turn out onto a floured surface and gather into a ball. Cover with plastic wrap and chill for 15 minutes. Preheat the oven to moderately hot 200°C (400°F/Gas 6). Grease a deep loose-based fluted flan tin measuring 19 cm (7½ inch) across the base.
2 Roll the pastry between 2 sheets of baking paper until large enough to line the flan tin. Fit the pastry into the tin and trim off any excess using a sharp knife. Prick the base with a fork and chill for 10 minutes. Place the flan tin on a heated baking tray and bake for 12 minutes, or until the pastry is just browned and dry. Leave to cool.
3 To make the filling, heat the oil in a pan and cook the onion, carrot, parsnip and cumin seeds, stirring over medium heat until the onion is translucent. Stir in the coriander and add salt to taste. Remove from the heat and cool slightly.
4 Crumble the cheese over the base of the pastry shell, then spoon the vegetable mixture over. Combine the eggs and cream in a small jug and pour over the vegetable mixture. Sprinkle the top with freshly ground black pepper. Bake for 45 minutes, or until set.

NUTRITION PER SERVE (6)
Protein 15 g; Fat 45 g; Carbohydrate 40 g; Dietary Fibre 7 g; Cholesterol 210 mg; 2560 kJ (610 cal)

Roll out the pastry until it is large enough to fit the prepared flan tin.

Leave the baked pastry shell on the baking tray to cool.

Spoon the vegetable mixture over the cheese in the base of the quiche.

ASPARAGUS AND PARMESAN QUICHE

Preparation time: 25 minutes
  + 50 minutes refrigeration
Total cooking time: 1 hour
Serves 4

1¹/₂ cups (185 g/6 oz) plain flour
125 g (4 oz) cold butter, chopped
1 egg yolk

Asparagus Filling
¹/₂ cup (50 g/1³/₄ oz) freshly
  grated Parmesan
30 g (1 oz) butter
1 small red onion, chopped
2 spring onions, chopped
1 tablespoon chopped dill
1 tablespoon chopped chives
1 egg, lightly beaten
¹/₄ cup (60 ml/2 fl oz) sour
  cream
¹/₄ cup (60 ml/2 fl oz) cream
400 g (13 oz) canned asparagus,
  drained

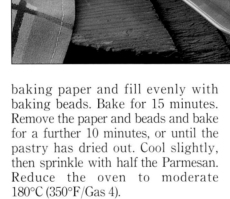

1 Process the flour and butter for about 15 seconds until crumbly. Add the egg yolk and 2 tablespoons of water. Process in short bursts until the mixture just comes together. Add a little extra water if needed. Turn out onto a floured surface and gather into a ball. Cover with plastic wrap and chill for 30 minutes.
2 Roll the pastry between 2 sheets of baking paper until it is large enough to fit and overlap a 35 x 10 cm (14 x 4 inch) rectangular loose-based flan tin. Line the flan tin and trim off any excess pastry using a sharp knife. Chill for 20 minutes. Preheat the oven to moderately hot 190°C (375°F/Gas 5). Cover the pastry with baking paper and fill evenly with baking beads. Bake for 15 minutes. Remove the paper and beads and bake for a further 10 minutes, or until the pastry has dried out. Cool slightly, then sprinkle with half the Parmesan. Reduce the oven to moderate 180°C (350°F/Gas 4).
3 To make the asparagus filling, melt the butter in a pan and cook the onions for 2–3 minutes until soft. Stir in the herbs and cool. Whisk together the egg, sour cream, cream and remaining Parmesan and season.
4 Spread the onion mixture over the pastry, lay the asparagus spears over the top and add the egg mixture. Bake for 25–30 minutes, or until golden.

NUTRITION PER SERVE
Protein 15 g; Fat 50 g; Carbohydrate 35 g; Dietary Fibre 4 g; Cholesterol 240 mg; 2800 kJ (665 cal)

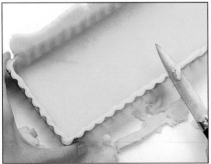

Trim the excess pastry from the edge of the tin using a sharp knife.

Whisk together the egg, sour cream, cream and remaining Parmesan.

Arrange the asparagus evenly over the top of the quiche.

LEEK AND HAM QUICHE WITH POLENTA PASTRY

Preparation time: 45 minutes
+ 50 minutes refrigeration
Total cooking time: 1 hour 15 minutes
Serves 6

1 cup (125 g/4 oz) plain flour
1/2 cup (75 g/2 1/2 oz) polenta
90 g (3 oz) butter, chopped
90 g (3 oz) cream cheese,
  chopped

Leek and Ham Filling
50 g (1 3/4 oz) butter
2 leeks, thinly sliced
2 eggs, lightly beaten
1 cup (250 ml/8 fl oz) cream
1/2 teaspoon ground nutmeg
100 g (3 1/2 oz) ham, chopped
75 g (2 1/2 oz) Swiss cheese,
  grated

1 Process the flour and polenta briefly to mix together. Add the butter and cream cheese and process for about 15 seconds until the mixture comes together. Add 1–2 tablespoons of water if needed. Turn out onto a floured surface and gather into a ball. Cover with plastic wrap and chill for 30 minutes.

2 To make the filling, heat the butter in a heavy-based pan. Add the leeks and cook, covered, stirring frequently for 10–15 minutes, or until soft but not brown. Cool. Mix together the beaten eggs, cream and nutmeg in a bowl. Season with pepper.

3 Grease a shallow 21 x 28 cm (8 1/2 x 11 inch) loose-based flan tin with melted butter. Roll the pastry between two sheets of baking paper until it is large enough to fit the tin.

Line the tin and trim off any excess pastry using a sharp knife. Chill for 20 minutes. Preheat the oven to moderately hot 190°C (375°F/Gas 5). Cover the pastry shell with baking paper and fill evenly with baking beads. Bake for 15 minutes. Remove the paper and beads and bake for a further 15 minutes, or until the pastry is dried out and cooked. Reduce the oven to moderate 180°C (350°F/Gas 4).

4 Spread the leek over the base of the pastry shell and sprinkle the ham and cheese over. Pour over the cream mixture. Bake for 30 minutes, or until golden brown and set.

NUTRITION PER SERVE
Protein 15 g; Fat 50 g; Carbohydrate 25 g; Dietary Fibre 2 g; Cholesterol 210 mg; 2495 kJ (595 cal)

Add the chopped butter and cream cheese to the flour and polenta.

Cook the leek, stirring frequently, until soft but not brown.

Sprinkle the top of the quiche with the ham and cheese.

29

FETA, BASIL AND BLACK OLIVE QUICHE

Preparation time: 40 minutes
  + 25 minutes refrigeration
Total cooking time: 40 minutes
Serves 6

1¼ cups (155 g/5 oz) self-
  raising flour, sifted
90 g (3 oz) butter, melted and
  cooled
¼ cup (60 ml/2 fl oz) milk

Filling
250 g (8 oz) feta cheese, cut
  into cubes
¼ cup (15 g/½ oz) basil leaves,
  shredded
¼ cup (30 g/1 oz) sliced black
  olives
3 eggs, lightly beaten
⅓ cup (80 ml/2¾ fl oz) milk
⅓ cup (90 g/3 oz) sour cream
semi-dried tomatoes, to serve
basil leaves, to serve

1 Grease a loose-based flan tin measuring 22 cm (8¾ inches) across the base. Place the flour in a large bowl and make a well in the centre. Add the butter and milk and stir until the mixture comes together to form a dough. Turn out onto a floured surface and gather into a ball. Refrigerate for 5 minutes. Roll out the pastry and place in the tin, pressing it well into the sides. Trim off any excess pastry. Refrigerate for 20 minutes. Preheat the oven to moderately hot 200°C (400°F/Gas 6).
2 To make the filling, spread the cubes of feta evenly over the base of the pastry and top with the shredded basil and olives. Whisk the eggs, milk and sour cream together until smooth, then pour into the pastry shell. Bake for 15 minutes, reduce the oven to moderate 180°C (350°F/Gas 4) and cook for a further 25 minutes, or until the filling is firmly set.
3 Cut the semi-dried tomatoes in half and toss with the basil. Serve the quiche at room temperature, with a spoonful of tomato and basil.

NUTRITION PER SERVE
Protein 15 g; Fat 35 g; Carbohydrate 20 g;
Dietary Fibre 2 g; Cholesterol 180 mg;
1750 kJ (415 cal)

Cut the feta into cubes and shred the basil leaves.

Add the melted butter and milk to the well in the centre of the flour.

Sprinkle the shredded basil and sliced olives over the top of the quiche.

Cut the semi-dried tomatoes in half using a sharp knife.

ASPARAGUS AND ARTICHOKE QUICHES

Preparation time: 40 minutes
  + 30 minutes refrigeration
Total cooking time: 40 minutes
Makes 6

1¼ cups (155 g/5 oz) plain flour
90 g (3 oz) cold butter, chopped
½ cup (60 g/2 oz) grated
    Cheddar

Filling
1 bunch (155 g/5 oz) asparagus,
    trimmed, cut into bite-sized
    pieces
2 eggs
⅓ cup (80 ml/2¾ fl oz) cream
⅓ cup (40 g/1¼ oz) grated
    Gruyère cheese
140 g (4½ oz) marinated
    artichoke hearts, quartered

1 Process the flour and butter for about 15 seconds until crumbly. Add the cheese and 2–3 tablespoons of water. Process in short bursts until the mixture comes together. Add a little extra water if needed. Turn out onto a floured surface and gather into a ball. Cover with plastic wrap and refrigerate for at least 30 minutes.
2 Preheat the oven to moderately hot 190°C (375°F/Gas 5). Grease 6 loose-based fluted flan tins measuring 8.5 cm (3¼ inches) across the base. Roll out the pastry and line the tins. Trim off any excess pastry with a sharp knife. Prick the pastry bases with a fork, place on a baking tray and bake for 10–12 minutes, or until the pastry is light and golden.
3 To make the filling, blanch the asparagus pieces in boiling salted water. Drain and refresh them in icy-cold water. Lightly beat the eggs, cream and cheese together and season with salt and black pepper.
4 Divide the artichokes and asparagus among the pastry shells, pour the egg and cream mixture over and sprinkle with cheese. Bake for 25 minutes, or until the filling is set and golden. If the pastry becomes too brown before the filling is fully set, cover with pieces of foil.

NUTRITION PER SERVE
Protein 10 g; Fat 30 g; Carbohydrate 20 g; Dietary Fibre 2 g; Cholesterol 150 mg; 1665 kJ (395 cal)

Cut the marinated artichoke hearts into quarters.

Process in short bursts until the mixture comes just together.

Divide the artichoke and asparagus evenly among the pastry shells.

SPINACH AND RED CAPSICUM QUICHES WITH CHIVE PASTRY

Preparation time: 40 minutes
+ 45 minutes refrigeration
Total cooking time: 1 hour 5 minutes
Makes 4

1¾ cups (215 g/7 oz) plain flour
2 tablespoons chopped chives
125 g (4 oz) cold butter, chopped
1 egg yolk

Spinach and Red Capsicum Filling
1 bunch (500 g/1 lb) English spinach
30 g (1 oz) butter
6 spring onions, finely sliced
1–2 cloves garlic, finely chopped
1 small red capsicum, finely chopped
2 eggs, lightly beaten
1 cup (250 ml/8 fl oz) cream
100 g (3½ oz) firm Camembert or Brie, cut into 8 slices

1 Place the flour and chives in a food processor, add the butter and process for about 15 seconds until the mixture is crumbly. Add the egg yolk and 3 tablespoons of water. Process in short bursts until the mixture just comes together. Add a little extra water if necessary. Turn out onto a floured surface and gather into a ball. Cover the pastry with plastic wrap and refrigerate for at least 30 minutes.
2 To make the spinach and red capsicum filling, wash the spinach thoroughly and remove the stalks. Place in a large pan, cover and cook over medium heat for 5 minutes, until it is wilted. Drain and allow to cool. Using your hands, squeeze as much moisture from the spinach as possible. Chop roughly.
3 Heat the butter in a pan and cook the spring onion, garlic and capsicum for 5–7 minutes, stirring frequently. Stir in the spinach and cool. Combine the eggs and cream in a small jug and season with salt and freshly ground black pepper.
4 Grease 4 loose-based fluted flan tins measuring 11 cm (4½ inches) across the base. Divide the pastry into 4 equal pieces and roll each to fit and overlap the prepared tins. Lift the pastry into the tins and press well into the edges. Trim the excess pastry from the edges with a sharp knife or by rolling a rolling pin across the top of the tins. Cover and refrigerate for a further 15 minutes. Preheat the oven to moderately hot 190°C (375°F/Gas 5). Cover the pastry shells with baking paper and fill evenly with baking beads or rice. Bake for 10 minutes. Remove the paper and rice and bake for a further 10 minutes.
5 Divide the spinach mixture evenly among the pastry shells. Pour the combined cream and egg mixture over the spinach. Place 2 slices of the cheese on top of each quiche. Bake for 25–30 minutes, or until the filling is golden brown and set.

NUTRITION PER QUICHE
Protein 15 g; Fat 45 g; Carbohydrate 30 g; Dietary Fibre 4 g; Cholesterol 230 mg; 2440 kJ (580 cal)

COOK'S FILE

Note: If you prefer, you can replace the Camembert or Brie with other cheeses such as a mature Cheddar, mozzarella or fontina. (Fontina is a semi-firm yet creamy cheese.)

Use a large, sharp knife to finely chop the garlic.

Cut the firm Camembert or Brie into 8 slices.

Turn the pastry mixture out onto a floured surface and gather into a ball.

Using your hand, squeeze as much moisture from the spinach as possible.

Cook the spring onion, garlic and capsicum, stirring frequently.

Cover the pastry shells with baking paper and fill evenly with rice.

SALMON AND SPRING ONION QUICHE

Preparation time: 20 minutes
 + 20 minutes refrigeration
Total cooking time: 55 minutes
Serves 6

2 cups (250 g/8 oz) self-raising
   flour
160 g (5½ oz) butter, melted
½ cup (125 ml/4 fl oz) milk

Filling
415 g (13¼ oz) can red salmon,
   drained and flaked
4 spring onions, sliced
⅓ cup (20 g/¾ oz) chopped
   parsley
4 eggs, lightly beaten
½ cup (125 ml/4 fl oz) milk
½ cup (125 ml/4 fl oz) cream
½ cup (60 g/2 oz) grated
   Cheddar

1 Grease a loose-based fluted flan tin measuring 26 cm (10½ inches) across the base. Sift the flour into a large bowl and make a well in the centre. Pour in the melted butter and milk and mix until the mixture comes together and forms a dough. Refrigerate for 20 minutes. Preheat the oven to moderately hot 200°C (400°F/Gas 6). Roll out the pastry and line the tin. Trim off any excess using a sharp knife or by rolling a rolling pin across the top of the tin.

2 Cover the pastry with baking paper and fill evenly with baking beads. Bake for 15 minutes. Remove the paper and beads and bake for 10 minutes. Cool. Reduce the oven to moderate 180°C (350°F/Gas 4).

3 Place the salmon in the pastry. Then combine the spring onions, parsley, eggs, milk, cream and cheese and pour over the filling. Bake for 30 minutes, or until set.

NUTRITION PER SERVE
Protein 20 g; Fat 35 g; Carbohydrate 20 g; Dietary Fibre 1 g; Cholesterol 210 mg; 1985 kJ (470 cal)

Break the drained red salmon into flakes using a fork.

Pour the melted butter and milk into the well in the sifted flour.

Mix together the spring onions, parsley, eggs, milk, cream and cheese.

EGGPLANT AND SUN-DRIED CAPSICUM QUICHES

Preparation time: 30 minutes
  + 45 minutes refrigeration
Total cooking time: 1 hour
Makes 6

1¹/2 cups (185 g/6 oz) plain
    flour
125 g (4 oz) cold butter, chopped
1 egg yolk

Filling
100 g (3¹/2 oz) eggplant, thinly
    sliced
30 g (1 oz) butter
4 spring onions, finely chopped
1–2 cloves garlic, crushed
¹/2 small red capsicum, finely
    chopped
¹/4 cup (40 g/1¹/4 oz) sun-dried
    capsicums, drained and
    chopped
2 eggs, lightly beaten
³/4 cup (185 ml/6 fl oz) cream

1 Process the flour and butter for about 15 seconds until crumbly. Add the egg yolk and 1 tablespoon of water. Process in short bursts until the mixture comes together. Add a little extra water if needed. Turn out onto a floured surface and gather into a ball. Cover with plastic wrap and refrigerate for at least 30 minutes.
2 To make the filling, brush the eggplant slices with olive oil and grill for 3 minutes on each side, until browned. Heat the butter in a pan and cook the spring onion, garlic and capsicum, stirring frequently, for 5 minutes, or until soft. Add the sun-dried capsicum and set aside to cool.

Combine the egg and cream and season with salt and pepper.
3 Grease 6 fluted flan tins measuring 8 cm (3 inches) across the base. Roll out the pastry thinly and line the tins, trimming off any excess. Cover and chill for 15 minutes. Preheat the oven to moderately hot 190°C (375°F/ Gas 5). Cover the pastry shells with baking paper and fill evenly with baking beads. Bake for 10 minutes.

Remove the paper and beads and bake for 10 minutes.
4 Divide the cooled filling mixture between the pastry shells, then top with the eggplant slices and pour over the cream and egg mixture. Bake for 25–30 minutes, or until set.

NUTRITION PER SERVE
Protein 7 g; Fat 35 g; Carbohydrate 25 g; Dietary Fibre 2 g; Cholesterol 200 mg; 1940 kJ (460 cal)

Cut the slender eggplant into thin slices on the diagonal.

Brush the sliced eggplant with oil and grill until browned.

Pour the cream and egg mixture over the filled quiches.

MEDITERRANEAN QUICHE

Preparation time: 50 minutes
  + 15 minutes refrigeration
Total cooking time: 1 hour 25 minutes
Serves 6–8

2 sheets ready-rolled shortcrust
  pastry

3 tablespoons olive oil
2 cloves garlic, crushed
1 medium onion, diced
1 small fresh chilli, seeded and
  finely chopped
1 red capsicum, chopped into
  bite-sized pieces
1 yellow capsicum, chopped into
  bite-sized pieces
400 g (13 oz) can tomatoes,
  drained and chopped
2 tablespoons chopped oregano
4 eggs, lightly beaten
1/3 cup (35 g/1 1/4 oz) freshly
  grated Parmesan

1 Grease a loose-based fluted flan tin measuring 22.5 cm (8 3/4 inches) across the base. Place the 2 sheets of pastry so that they are slightly overlapping and roll out until large enough to fit the prepared tin. Press well into the sides and trim off any excess using a sharp knife. Cover and chill for 15 minutes. Preheat the oven to moderately hot 190°C (375°F/Gas 5). Cover the pastry shell with baking paper and fill evenly with baking beads or rice. Bake for 10 minutes. Remove the paper and rice and bake for a further 10 minutes, or until golden. Cool on a wire rack.
2 Heat the oil and fry the garlic and onion until soft. Add the chilli, red and yellow capsicum and cook for 6 minutes. Stir in the tomatoes and oregano and simmer, covered, for 10 minutes. Remove the lid and cook until the liquid has evaporated. Remove from the heat and cool.
3 Stir the eggs and Parmesan into the tomato mixture and spoon into the pastry shell. Bake for 35–45 minutes, or until the filling has set.

NUTRITION PER SERVE (8)
Protein 9 g; Fat 25 g; Carbohydrate 20 g;
Dietary Fibre 2 g; Cholesterol 105 mg;
1345 kJ (320 cal)

Remove the baking paper and rice from the pastry shell.

Add the finely chopped chilli and cubed red and yellow capsicum.

Cook the vegetables until the liquid has evaporated.

Spoon the filling mixture evenly into the pastry case.

MUSTARD CHICKEN AND ASPARAGUS QUICHE

Preparation time: 25 minutes
+ 40 minutes refrigeration
Total cooking time: 1 hour 20 minutes
Serves 8

2 cups (250 g/8 oz) plain flour
100 g (3½ oz) cold butter, chopped
1 egg yolk

Filling
150 g (5 oz) asparagus, chopped
25 g (¾ oz) butter
1 onion, chopped
¼ cup (75 g/2½ oz) wholegrain mustard
200 g (6½ oz) soft cream cheese
½ cup (125 ml/4 fl oz) cream
3 eggs, lightly beaten
200 g (6½ oz) cooked chicken, chopped
½ teaspoon black pepper

1 Process the flour and butter until crumbly. Add the egg yolk and 3 tablespoons of water. Process in short bursts until the mixture comes together. Add a little extra water if needed. Turn onto a floured surface and gather into a ball. Cover with plastic wrap and chill for 30 minutes. Grease a deep loose-based flan tin measuring 19 cm (7½ inches) across the base.
2 Roll out the pastry and line the tin. Trim off any excess with a sharp knife. Place the flan tin on a baking tray and chill for 10 minutes. Preheat the oven to moderately hot 200°C (400°F/Gas 6). Cover the pastry with baking paper and fill evenly with

baking beads. Bake for 10 minutes. Remove the paper and beads and bake for about 10 minutes, until the pastry is lightly browned and dry. Cool. Reduce the oven to moderate 180°C (350°F/Gas 4).
3 To make the filling, boil or steam the asparagus until tender. Drain and pat dry with paper towels. Heat the butter in a pan and cook the onion until translucent. Remove from the heat and add the mustard and cream

cheese, stirring until the cheese has melted. Cool. Add the cream, eggs, chicken and asparagus and mix well.
4 Spoon the filling into the pastry shell and sprinkle with the pepper. Bake for 50 minutes–1 hour, or until puffed and set. Cool for at least 15 minutes before cutting.

NUTRITION PER SERVE
Protein 15 g; Fat 30 g; Carbohydrate 25 g; Dietary Fibre 2 g; Cholesterol 190 mg; 1860 kJ (440 cal)

When the mixture is crumbly add the egg yolk.

Dry the asparagus well to avoid excess moisture softening the quiche.

Add the mustard and cream cheese and stir until the cheese has melted.

HAM AND SWEETCORN PARTY QUICHES

Preparation time: 25 minutes
Total cooking time: 20 minutes
Makes 30

20 g (3/4 oz) butter
4 spring onions, finely chopped
100 g (31/2 oz) leg ham, cut in thin strips
270 g (9 oz) can corn kernels, drained
2 eggs, lightly beaten
2 tablespoons chopped chives

1/2 cup (125 ml/4 fl oz) cream
1/2 cup (125 ml/4 fl oz) milk

10 sheets filo pastry
oil or melted butter, for brushing

1 Preheat the oven to moderately hot 200°C (400°F/Gas 6). Melt the butter in a pan and cook the spring onion for 2 minutes, or until soft. Transfer to a bowl and add the ham, corn, egg and chives. Combine the cream and milk and stir in to the onion mixture.

2 Work with 5 sheets of pastry at a time, keeping the remainder covered with baking paper and a damp tea towel. Brush each sheet of pastry with oil or melted butter and pile them up into a stack. Using an 8 cm (3 inch) round cutter, cut 15 circles from the stacked sheets.

3 Place the pastry circles in greased shallow 6 cm (21/2 inch) round patty tins. Fill each circle of pastry with a tablespoon of filling. Repeat with the 5 remaining sheets of filo. Bake for 15–20 minutes, or until golden.

NUTRITION PER QUICHE
Protein 2 g; Fat 4 g; Carbohydrate 4 g; Dietary Fibre 0 g; Cholesterol 20 mg; 255 kJ (60 cal)

Stir the combined cream and milk into the spring onion and ham mixture.

Cover the pastry with baking paper and a damp tea towel to prevent it drying out.

Fill each circle of pastry with a tablespoon of filling.

FRESH HERB QUICHE

Preparation time: 30 minutes
  + 50 minutes refrigeration
Total cooking time: 1 hour
Serves 4–6

1¹/2 cups (185 g/6 oz) plain flour
¹/4 cup (15 g/¹/2 oz) chopped
    parsley
125 g (4 oz) cold butter, chopped
1 egg yolk

Herb Filling
30 g (1 oz) butter
1 small leek, thinly sliced
1–2 cloves garlic, crushed
4 spring onions, chopped
¹/4 cup (15 g/¹/2 oz) chopped
    parsley
2 tablespoons chopped chives
2 tablespoons chopped dill
2 tablespoons oregano leaves
3 eggs
1 cup (250 ml/8 fl oz) cream
¹/4 cup (60 ml/2 fl oz) milk
1 cup (125 g/4 oz) grated
    Cheddar

1 Process the flour, parsley and butter until crumbly. Add the egg yolk and 1 tablespoon of water. Process in short bursts until the mixture comes together. Add a little extra water if needed. Turn out onto a floured surface and gather into a ball. Cover with plastic wrap and chill for 30 minutes.
2 Grease a loose-based flan tin measuring 24 cm (9¹/2 inches) across the base. Roll out the pastry, line the prepared tin and trim off any excess. Chill the lined flan tin for 20 minutes. Preheat the oven to moderately hot 190°C (375°F/Gas 5). Cover the pastry

with baking paper and fill with baking beads. Bake for 15 minutes. Remove the paper and beads and bake for a further 10 minutes. Reduce the oven to moderate 180°C (350°F/Gas 4).
3 To make the filling, heat the butter in a heavy-based pan. Cook the leek, garlic and spring onion for 10 minutes, stirring frequently until cooked. Add the herbs and cool.

4 Beat the eggs, cream and milk and season with pepper. Spread the leek and herb mixture over the base of the pastry. Pour over the egg mixture and sprinkle with the Cheddar. Bake for 25–30 minutes, or until golden.

NUTRITION PER SERVE (6)
Protein 15 g; Fat 45 g; Carbohydrate 25 g; Dietary Fibre 2 g; Cholesterol 220 mg; 2300 kJ (545 cal)

When the mixture is crumbly, add the egg yolk and water.

When the leek is cooked, stir through the herbs.

Sprinkle the grated Cheddar over the top of the quiche.

PIES

TRADITIONAL MEAT PIE

Preparation time: 30 minutes
  + overnight refrigeration
Total cooking time: 3 hours 30 minutes
Serves 4

750 g (1¹/₂ lb) gravy beef
¹/₃ cup (40 g/1¹/₄ oz) plain flour
¹/₃ cup (80 ml/2³/₄ fl oz) oil
3 onions, sliced
2 cups (500 ml/16 fl oz) beef
  stock
1 tablespoon Worcestershire
  sauce
2 tablespoons chopped parsley

1 sheet ready-rolled shortcrust
  pastry
1 sheet ready-rolled puff pastry
1 egg yolk, to glaze

1 Cut the beef into chunks. Season the flour with salt and freshly ground black pepper and place in a plastic bag. Add the meat and shake to coat with flour. Shake off any excess. Heat a little of the oil in a large heavy-based pan and cook the meat, in batches, until golden brown. Remove from the pan.
2 Add the onion to the pan and cook over low heat until golden and translucent. Return the meat to the pan, add the stock and Worcestershire sauce and stir well. Bring to the boil, then reduce the heat, cover and simmer gently for 2–2¹/₂ hours, or until the meat is very tender. You will need to stir the meat every 30 minutes to prevent sticking. Stir in the parsley. Remove from the pan and leave to cool completely, then refrigerate (preferably overnight).
3 Place a baking tray in the oven and preheat to hot 220°C (425°F/Gas 7). Grease a deep 20 cm (8 inch) round pie plate. Use the shortcrust pastry to line the bottom and sides of the dish. You may need to roll the square of pastry a little larger to fit into the prepared dish. Place the cold filling into the pastry shell.
4 Mix the egg yolk with 2 teaspoons of water and use to brush the rim of the pastry shell. Place the puff pastry over the top of the filling, press the edges gently to seal, then trim away the extra pastry. Pinch or crimp the edges to decorate. Cut two small slits in the pastry to allow the steam to escape during cooking. Brush with the beaten egg yolk mixture. Place the pie on the preheated tray and bake for 20 minutes. Reduce the heat to moderate 180°C (350°F/Gas 4) and cook for a further 15–20 minutes. Check the pastry during cooking; if it is well browned, cover with a piece of foil for the remaining time.

NUTRITION PER SERVE
Protein 50 g; Fat 55 g; Carbohydrate 45 g; Dietary Fibre 3 g; Cholesterol 180 mg; 3535 kJ (840 cal)

To coat the meat, place it in a plastic bag with the seasoned flour and shake well.

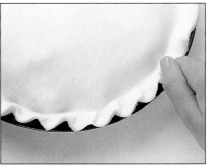

Pinch or crimp the edges of the pie for a decorative finish.

FILO VEGETABLE STRUDEL

Preparation time: 30 minutes
 + 30 minutes standing
Total cooking time: 1 hour 10 minutes
Serves 6–8

1 large eggplant, sliced
1 red capsicum
3 zucchini, sliced lengthways
2 tablespoons olive oil
6 sheets filo pastry
50 g (1¾ oz) baby English
　　spinach leaves
60 g (2 oz) feta cheese, sliced

1 Preheat the oven to moderately hot 190°C (375°F/Gas 5). Sprinkle the eggplant slices with a little salt and leave to drain in a colander for 30 minutes. Pat dry with paper towels.
2 Cut the capsicum into quarters and remove the seeds. Place, skin-side-up, under a medium grill for 10 minutes, or until soft and lightly browned, and then peel the skins away. Brush the eggplant and zucchini slices with olive oil and grill for 5–10 minutes, or until golden brown. Set aside to cool.
3 Brush one sheet of filo pastry at a time with olive oil, then lay them on top of each other. Place half the eggplant slices lengthways down the

centre of the filo, top with a layer of zucchini, capsicum, spinach and feta cheese. Repeat the layers until the vegetables and cheese are used up. Tuck in the ends of the pastry, then roll up like a parcel; brush lightly with oil and place on a baking tray. Bake for 35 minutes, or until golden brown.

NUTRITION PER SERVE (8)
Protein 4 g; Fat 7 g; Carbohydrate 9 g;
Dietary Fibre 3 g; Cholesterol 5 mg;
485 kJ (115 cal)

COOK'S FILE

Note: Unopened filo can be stored in the refrigerator for up to a month. Once opened, use within 2–3 days.

Cut a large eggplant into thin slices with a sharp knife.

Build up layers of eggplant, zucchini, capsicum, spinach and feta cheese.

Tuck in the ends of the pastry, then roll up like a parcel to make a strudel.

SALMON AND LEEK PIE

Preparation time: 40 minutes
Total cooking time: 55 minutes
Serves 4

20 g (³/4 oz) butter
2 leeks, sliced
410 g (13 oz) can red salmon,
    drained
1 tablespoon chopped oregano
2 tablespoons chopped parsley
1 egg
³/4 cup (185 ml/6 fl oz) milk
2 sheets ready-rolled puff pastry
1 egg, lightly beaten, to glaze

1 Preheat the oven to moderately hot 200°C (400°F/Gas 6). Melt the butter in a pan and fry the leeks over low heat for 10 minutes, or until soft and golden, but do not allow to brown.
2 Grease the base of a shallow 20 cm (8 inch) oven dish. Flake the salmon in a small bowl and mix with the herbs. Spread half the salmon over the base of the dish and cover with the leeks. Arrange the remaining salmon over the top.
3 Lightly whisk the egg and milk together and season to taste. Pour over the salmon and leek filling. Cover with 1 sheet of the pastry. If the rim of your dish is a little wider, you may

need to roll out the pastry a little. Trim the excess edges with a sharp knife and brush with the beaten egg. Make a few slits in the pastry to allow the steam to escape.
4 Cut the remaining sheet of pastry into leaf shapes and use a sharp knife to mark in veins. Use these to decorate the top of the pie. Then brush with more egg. Bake for 35–45 minutes, or until the pastry is puffed and golden. If the pastry starts to overbrown, cover with a piece of foil. Serve warm.

NUTRITION PER SERVE
Protein 35 g; Fat 40 g; Carbohydrate 35 g;
Dietary Fibre 3 g; Cholesterol 205 mg;
2600 kJ (620 cal)

Fry the leeks over low heat until they are soft and golden.

Make a layer with half the salmon and herb mixture and cover with the leeks.

Decorate the top of the pie with leaf shapes cut from the second pastry sheet.

CHICKEN CORIANDER PIE

Preparation time: 40 minutes
Total cooking time: 45 minutes
Serves 4

50 g (1³/4 oz) butter
2 onions, chopped
100 g (3¹/2 oz) button
    mushrooms, sliced
250 g (8 oz) cooked chicken,
    roughly chopped
4 hard-boiled eggs
1 tablespoon plain flour
280 ml (9 fl oz) chicken stock
1 egg yolk
3 tablespoons chopped
    coriander
250 g (8 oz) block or packet
    puff pastry
1 egg, lightly beaten, to glaze

1 Melt half of the butter in a large pan. Add the onion and mushrooms and sauté for about 5 minutes, or until soft, then stir in the chicken. Spoon half of the mixture into a 20 cm (8 inch) round, straight-sided pie dish. Slice the eggs and lay over the chicken. Top with the remaining mixture.

2 Preheat the oven to moderately hot 200°C (400°F/Gas 6). Melt the remaining butter in a pan, add the flour and cook for 1 minute. Gradually add the stock and cook for 4 minutes, stirring constantly, then remove from the heat. Stir in the egg yolk and coriander, and season with salt and freshly ground black pepper. Allow the mixture to cool before pouring over the chicken filling.

3 Roll out the pastry into a square larger than the pie dish. Dampen the dish rim with water and lay the pastry over, pressing down firmly to seal. Trim the edges and roll out the leftover pastry into a long strip. Slice it into 3 equal lengths and make a plait. Brush the top of the pie with beaten egg and place the plait around the edge. Brush again with beaten egg. Make a few slits in the centre and bake for 35 minutes, or until golden.

NUTRITION PER SERVE
Protein 25 g; Fat 35 g; Carbohydrate 30 g; Dietary Fibre 3 g; Cholesterol 385 mg; 2220 kJ (530 cal)

Add the chicken to the cooked onion and mushrooms in the pan.

Slice the hard-boiled eggs and arrange them over the chicken filling.

Stir the egg yolk and coriander into the heated stock and flour.

Lay the decorative plait around the edge of the pie.

CHEESE 'N' TATTIE PIE

Preparation time: 45 minutes
Total cooking time: 40 minutes
Serves 6–8

1 kg (2 lb) new potatoes, cooked
   and sliced
1 cup (125 g/4 oz) grated
   Cheddar
1 clove garlic, crushed
2 tablespoons chopped chives
2 tablespoons chopped
   marjoram
5 thin rashers bacon
1/3 cup (80 ml/2³/4 fl oz) thick
   cream

2 eggs
2 sheets ready-rolled puff
   pastry
1 egg yolk, beaten, to glaze

1 Preheat the oven to hot 220°C (425°F/Gas 7). Place half the potatoes, overlapping the slices, in the base of a large dish, and season generously with salt and freshly ground black pepper. Sprinkle over half the cheese, garlic, chives and marjoram. Trim the rind off the bacon and arrange the rashers over the cheese and herbs. Top with the remaining potato, cheese, garlic, chives and marjoram. Pour over the mixed cream and eggs.

2 Cut each pastry sheet into quarters, and each quarter into 3 equal lengths. Place the strips, overlapping, around the top of the pie, leaving the centre open. Press down the edges so that the pastry sticks to the pie dish, then trim the edge. Combine the egg yolk with a little water and brush the top of the pie.

3 Bake for 15 minutes; reduce the heat to moderate 180°C (350°F/Gas 4), and bake for a further 15–20 minutes, or until the pastry is puffed and golden and the filling is set. Allow to stand for 10 minutes before serving.

NUTRITION PER SERVE (8)
Protein 15 g; Fat 20 g; Carbohydrate 30 g; Dietary Fibre 3 g; Cholesterol 115 mg; 1620 kJ (385 cal)

Top with the remaining potato slices, cheese, garlic, marjoram and chives.

Overlap the pastry strips around the top of the pie, leaving the centre open.

Brush the top of the pie with a little combined egg yolk and water.

THAI GREEN CURRY CHICKEN PIES

Preparation time: 45 minutes
  + 30 minutes refrigeration
Total cooking time: 45 minutes
Serves 4

1 cup (125 g/4 oz) plain flour
65 g (2¼ oz) cold butter, chopped

Filling
200 g (6½ oz) green beans
1 tablespoon oil
1 tablespoon Thai green curry paste
½ cup (125 ml/4 fl oz) coconut milk
500 g (1 lb) chicken thigh fillets, cut into bite-sized pieces
2 kaffir lime leaves
2 teaspoons fish sauce
1 tablespoon lime juice
2 teaspoons soft brown sugar
1 tablespoon cornflour
1 tablespoon water
1 egg, lightly beaten, to glaze

1 Process the flour and butter in a food processor until the mixture resembles fine breadcrumbs. Add 1–2 tablespoons of cold water. Process in short bursts until the mixture just comes together, adding a little extra water if necessary. Turn out onto a lightly floured surface and quickly bring together into a ball. Cover with plastic wrap and refrigerate for at least 30 minutes.
2 Cut the beans into short lengths. Heat the oil in a wok or heavy-based frying pan. Add the curry paste and cook for 1 minute, stirring constantly.

Add the coconut milk and ¼ cup (60 ml/2 fl oz) of water and bring to the boil. Add the chicken, beans and kaffir lime leaves and stir through. Simmer gently for 15 minutes, or until the chicken is cooked. Add the fish sauce, lime juice and sugar. In a small bowl mix together the cornflour and 1 tablespoon of water to a smooth consistency. Add to the curry and stir constantly until the sauce thickens and begins to bubble. Remove the kaffir lime leaves, and divide the mixture between four ½ cup- (125 ml/ 4 fl oz) capacity ramekins.

3 Divide the pastry into 4 equal pieces. Roll each piece between two sheets of baking paper until it is slightly larger than the top of the ramekins. Brush the edges of the ramekins with beaten egg and cover with the pastry. Press the edges around the rim to seal. Trim off any excess pastry using a sharp knife or by rolling a rolling pin across the top of the tin. Decorate the edges with the end of a teaspoon. Cut a small air hole in the top of each pie to allow the steam to escape during cooking. Brush with beaten egg. Place the ramekins on a baking tray and bake for 20–25 minutes, or until the pastry is golden brown. Serve immediately.

NUTRITION PER SERVE
Protein 35 g; Fat 30 g; Carbohydrate 30 g; Dietary Fibre 3 g; Cholesterol 175 mg; 2225 kJ (530 cal)

COOK'S FILE

Note: Coconut milk varies greatly in quality. You may get a 'curdled' or 'split' appearance, however this will not effect the flavour.
Hint: Dried kaffir lime leaves can be stored for up to 1 year if kept in a sealed plastic bag.

Cook the curry paste for 1 minute, then add the coconut milk.

Add the chicken, beans and kaffir lime leaves to the wok or pan.

Add the cornflour mixture to the curry and stir until it thickens and bubbles.

Remove the kaffir lime leaves before spooning the mixture into the ramekins.

Roll out each piece of pastry and place over the top of the ramekins.

Glaze the pastry crusts with a little beaten egg to give a golden finish.

SWEET POTATO, PUMPKIN AND COCONUT LATTICE PIES

Preparation time: 45 minutes
+ 20 minutes refrigeration
Total cooking time: 55 minutes
Makes 8

2 tablespoons oil
1 onion, finely chopped
2 cloves garlic, crushed
1 teaspoon grated fresh ginger
1 small red chilli, chopped
250 g (8 oz) orange sweet
    potato, peeled and cubed
250 g (8 oz) pumpkin, peeled
    and cubed
1/2 teaspoon fennel seeds
1/2 teaspoon yellow mustard
    seeds
1/2 teaspoon ground turmeric
1/2 teaspoon ground cumin
140 g (41/2 oz) can coconut milk
1/4 cup (15 g/1/2 oz) chopped
    coriander
4 sheets ready-rolled puff
    pastry
1 egg yolk, to glaze

1 Heat the oil in a pan and cook the onion, garlic, ginger and chilli for 5 minutes, stirring continuously, until the onion is cooked. Add the sweet potato, pumpkin, fennel and mustard seeds, turmeric and cumin. Stir for 2 minutes, then add the coconut milk and 2 tablespoons of water. Cook over low heat, stirring frequently, for 20 minutes, or until the vegetables are tender. Stir through the coriander and set aside to cool.
2 Grease a large baking tray. Cut eight 9.5 cm (33/4 inch) circles from 2 sheets of the pastry and place them on the tray. Divide the mixture between the circles and spread to within 1 cm (1/2 inch) of the edge. Mound the filling slightly in the centre. Brush the edges of the pastry with a little water.
3 Using a lattice cutter or a sharp knife, mark the remaining 2 sheets of pastry, and cut out eight 10 cm (4 inch) circles. Carefully open out the lattices and fit them over the mixture. Press the edges together firmly to seal. Using the back of a knife, press the outside edge lightly at 1 cm (1/2 inch) intervals. Refrigerate for at least 20 minutes. Preheat the oven to moderately hot 190°C (375°F/Gas 5). Mix the egg yolk with 1 teaspoon of water and brush the pastry. Bake for 20–25 minutes, or until golden.

NUTRITION PER SERVE
Protein 7 g; Fat 30 g; Carbohydrate 40 g; Dietary Fibre 3 g; Cholesterol 45 mg; 1800 kJ (430 cal)

Cut the orange sweet potato and pumpkin into cubes.

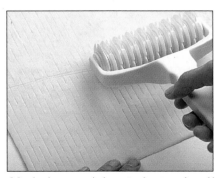

Mark the remaining 2 sheets of puff pastry with a lattice cutter.

Open out the lattices, fit them over the filling and press the edges to seal.

Finely chop the onion and dice the celery and carrot.

Once the onion is cooked; add the celery and carrot to the pan.

Remove the lid to allow the liquid to reduce to a thick sauce.

Mash the potato with the butter and milk until the mixture is smooth and fluffy.

SHEPHERD'S PIE

Preparation time: 25 minutes
Total cooking time: 2 hours
Serves 4–6

30 g (1 oz) butter
1 large onion, finely chopped
1 stick celery, finely diced
1 carrot, finely diced
2 teaspoons olive oil
1 kg (2 lb) lamb mince
1 tablespoon plain flour
1 1/2 cups (375 ml/12 fl oz) beef stock
1 teaspoon dried mixed herbs
1/2 teaspoon dried thyme
1 tablespoon tomato paste
2 teaspoons soft brown sugar
2 teaspoons red wine vinegar

Topping
1 kg (2 lb) potatoes, quartered
50 g (1 3/4 oz) butter
1/3 cup (80 ml/2 3/4 fl oz) milk
65 g (2 1/4 oz) grated Cheddar cheese

1 Melt the butter in a large pan and cook the onion over low heat until soft and golden. Add the celery and carrot; cook for a few more minutes. Remove from the pan and set aside. Heat the olive oil in the pan and quickly brown the mince in batches. Return all the meat to the pan.

2 Add the flour and cook for 1 minute. Return the onion mixture to the pan and stir in the stock, herbs, tomato paste, sugar and vinegar. Bring to the boil, reduce the heat, and simmer, covered, for about 1 hour. Towards the end of the cooking time, remove the lid to reduce the liquid to a thick sauce. Season with salt and freshly ground black pepper. Transfer to a casserole dish. Preheat the oven to moderate 180°C (350°F/Gas 4).

3 To make the topping, cook the potatoes in a large pan of boiling water until very tender. Drain; add the butter and milk and mash until smooth and fluffy. Spoon over the meat and fluff up with a fork. Scatter the top with grated cheese and bake for 35–40 minutes, or until golden.

NUTRITION PER SERVE (6)
Protein 40 g; Fat 40 g; Carbohydrate 30 g; Dietary Fibre 4 g; Cholesterol 165 mg; 2730 kJ (650 cal)

TOMATO AND GOAT'S CHEESE PIE

Preparation time: 30 minutes
 + 20 minutes refrigeration
Total cooking time: 30 minutes
Serves 6

1¹/₂ cups (185 g/6 oz) plain flour
100 g (3¹/₂ oz) cold butter,
  chopped
3 tablespoons grated mature
  Cheddar

Filling
1 egg yolk, lightly beaten
3 tablespoons dried
  breadcrumbs
4–5 tomatoes, sliced
100 g (3¹/₂ oz) goat's cheese
1 tablespoon olive oil
2 tablespoons small basil leaves
  or shredded basil

1 Place the flour and butter in a food processor and process until crumbly. Add the Cheddar, ¹/₂ teaspoon of salt and 2–3 tablespoons of water. Process in short bursts until the mixture just comes together, adding a little extra water if necessary. Turn the mixture out onto a floured surface and quickly bring it together into a ball. Cover the pastry with plastic wrap and refrigerate for at least 20 minutes.
2 Preheat the oven to moderate 180°C (350°F/Gas 4). Roll out the pastry on a lightly floured surface into a circle about 35 cm (14 inches) in diameter. Wrap the pastry around a rolling pin and carefully lift it onto a greased baking tray and then carefully unroll the pastry.
3 Brush most of the egg yolk lightly over the pastry and sprinkle with the breadcrumbs. Arrange the slices of tomato on the pastry so that they overlap in a circle leaving a wide border. Crumble the goat's cheese over the top of the tomatoes. Turn the edge of the pastry in over the tomato filling, and brush with the remaining egg yolk (mix with a little milk if there's not much egg left).
4 Bake for 30 minutes, or until the pastry is golden and the cheese has melted. Then drizzle with the olive oil and season well with salt and freshly ground black pepper. Scatter the top of the pie with the basil leaves, to serve.

NUTRITION PER SERVE
Protein 10 g; Fat 25 g; Carbohydrate 30 g; Dietary Fibre 3 g; Cholesterol 95 mg; 1620 kJ (385 cal)

Process the flour and butter until crumbly, then add the cheese.

Lay the slices of tomato on the pastry and breadcrumbs so that they overlap.

Turn the pastry edges in over the tomato and goat's cheese filling.

50

MOROCCAN CHICKEN FILO PIE

Preparation time: 40 minutes
Total cooking time: 40 minutes
Serves 4–6

1 tablespoon olive oil
1 red onion, chopped
2–3 cloves garlic, crushed
2 teaspoons grated fresh ginger
1 teaspoon ground turmeric
1 teaspoon ground cumin
1 teaspoon ground coriander
500 g (1 lb) cooked chicken, shredded
60 g (2 oz) slivered almonds, toasted
1 cup (50 g/1¾ oz) chopped coriander
⅓ cup (20 g/¾ oz) chopped parsley
1 teaspoon grated lemon rind
2 tablespoons stock or water
1 egg, lightly beaten
9 sheets filo pastry
50 g (1¾ oz) butter, melted
1 teaspoon caster sugar
¼ teaspoon ground cinnamon

1 Heat the oil in a large heavy-based frying pan and cook the onion, garlic and ginger, stirring, for 5 minutes, or until the onion is soft. Stir in the turmeric, cumin and coriander and cook, stirring, for 1–2 minutes. Remove from the heat; stir in the chicken, almonds, coriander, parsley and lemon rind. Leave to cool for 5 minutes, then stir in the stock or water and the beaten egg.

2 Preheat the oven to moderate 180°C (350°F/Gas 4). Grease a baking tray. Cut 6 sheets of filo into approximately 30 cm (12 inch) squares, retaining the extra strips. Cut each of the remaining sheets into 3 equal strips. Cover with a damp cloth. Brush 1 square with the melted butter and place on the baking tray. Lay another square at an angle on top and brush with melted butter. Repeat with the other squares to form a rough 8-pointed star. Spoon the chicken mixture into the centre, leaving a 5 cm (2 inch) border.

3 Turn the pastry edge in over the filling, leaving the centre open. Brush the pastry strips with melted butter and lightly scrunch and lay them over the top of the pie. Sprinkle with the combined caster sugar and cinnamon. Bake for 25 minutes, or until the pastry is cooked and golden brown.

NUTRITION PER SERVE (6)
Protein 30 g; Fat 20 g; Carbohydrate 15 g; Dietary Fibre 2 g; Cholesterol 130 mg; 1510 kJ (360 cal)

Gently shred the chicken pieces with your fingers.

Gather the edges of the pastry squares up over the chicken mixture.

Lightly scrunch the remaining strips and arrange them around the pie top.

FISHERMAN'S PIE

Preparation time: 40 minutes
Total cooking time: 1 hour
Serves 4

800 g (1 lb 10 oz) white fish
   fillets
1½ cups (375 ml/12 fl oz) milk
1 onion, roughly chopped
2 cloves
50 g (1¾ oz) butter
2 tablespoons plain flour
pinch of ground nutmeg
2 tablespoons chopped parsley
1 cup (155 g/5 oz) peas
750 g (1½ lb) potatoes,
   quartered
2 tablespoons hot milk
3 tablespoons grated Cheddar

1 Place the fish fillets in a pan and cover with the milk. Add the onion and cloves and bring to the boil. Reduce the heat and simmer for about 5 minutes, or until the fish is cooked; the flesh should be opaque and flake easily with a fork.

2 Preheat the oven to moderate 180°C (350°F/Gas 4). Remove the fish from the pan, reserving the milk and onion. Discard the cloves. Allow the fish to cool then remove any skin and bones and flake into bite-sized pieces with a fork.

3 Heat half of the butter in a pan, stir in the flour and cook, stirring, for 1 minute. Remove from the heat, add the reserved milk mixture and stir until smooth. Return to the heat and cook, stirring, until the sauce begins to bubble. Cook for another minute. Remove from the heat, allow to cool slightly, then add the nutmeg, parsley and peas. Season well with salt and freshly ground black pepper and gently fold in the fish. Spoon into a 5-cup (1.25 litre) capacity baking dish.

4 Cook the potatoes in a pan of boiling water until tender. Drain and add the milk and remaining butter. Mash until very smooth. Add the cheese; if the mixture is very stiff you may need to add a little more milk—the mixture should be fairly firm.

5 Spoon the potato mixture into a piping bag and pipe over the filling; or alternatively, spoon over the top of the filling and rough up with a fork. Bake for about 30 minutes, or until heated through.

NUTRITION PER SERVE
Protein 55 g; Fat 25 g; Carbohydrate 40 g; Dietary Fibre 6 g; Cholesterol 200 mg; 2565 kJ (610 cal)

Cover the fish fillets with the milk and add the onion and cloves.

Heat half the butter in a pan and stir in the flour.

Pipe the potato mixture across the pie until the top is completely covered.

BRIK A L'OEUF

Preparation time: 30 minutes
Total cooking time: 15 minutes
Serves 2

6 sheets filo pastry
30 g (1 oz) butter, melted
1 small onion, finely chopped
200 g (6½ oz) can tuna in oil, drained
6 stoned black olives, chopped
1 tablespoon finely chopped parsley
2 eggs

1 Preheat the oven to moderately hot 200°C (400°F/Gas 6). Cut the pastry sheets in half widthways. Brush 4 sheets with melted butter and lay them on top of each other. Place half of the combined onion, tuna, olives and parsley at one end and make a well in the centre. Break an egg into the well, being careful to leave it whole. Season with salt and freshly ground black pepper.

2 Brush 2 more sheets with melted butter, place them together and lay them on top of the tuna and egg. Fold in the sides and roll up into a neat firm package, still keeping the egg

whole. Place on a baking tray and brush with melted butter. Repeat with the remaining pastry and filling.

3 Bake for 15 minutes, or until the pastry is golden. Serve warm.

NUTRITION PER SERVE
Protein 35 g; Fat 35 g; Carbohydrate 25 g; Dietary Fibre 1 g; Cholesterol 260 mg; 2295 kJ (545 cal)

COOK'S FILE

Note: The yolk is still soft after 15 minutes cooking. If you prefer a firmer egg, bake for longer. Tuna in oil is preferable to brine as it will keep the filling moist when cooked.

Carefully break an egg into the centre of the tuna mixture.

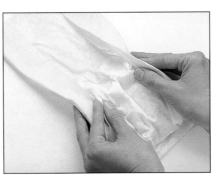

Lay an extra 2 sheets of filo over the tuna and egg and fold in the sides.

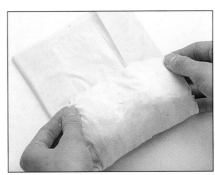

Roll up the pastry into a neat firm package, keeping the egg intact.

CHICKEN AND LEEK COBBLER

Preparation time: 1 hour
Total cooking time: 1 hour
Serves 4–6

50 g (1³/4 oz) butter
1 kg (2 lb) chicken breast
    fillets, cut into thick strips
1 large (225 g/7 oz) leek,
    trimmed and finely sliced
1 stick celery, finely sliced
1 tablespoon plain flour
1 cup (250 ml/8 fl oz) chicken
    stock
1 cup (250 ml/8 fl oz) cream
3 teaspoons Dijon mustard
3 teaspoons drained and rinsed
    green peppercorns

Topping
400 g (13 oz) potatoes,
    quartered
1¹/3 cups (165 g/5¹/2 oz) self-
    raising flour
¹/2 teaspoon salt
¹/4 cup (30 g/1 oz) grated
    mature Cheddar
100 g (3¹/2 oz) cold butter,
    chopped
1 egg yolk, lightly beaten, to
    glaze

1 Melt half the butter in a pan. When it begins to foam, add the chicken and cook until golden. Remove from the pan. Add the remaining butter and cook the leek and celery over medium heat until soft. Return the chicken to the pan.
2 Sprinkle the flour over the chicken and stir for about 1 minute. Remove from the heat and stir in the stock and cream. Mix well, making sure that there are no lumps. Return to the heat. Bring to the boil, then reduce the heat and simmer for about 20 minutes. Add the mustard and peppercorns and season to taste with salt and freshly ground black pepper. Transfer the mixture to a 1.25–1.5 litre capacity casserole dish and allow to cool. Preheat the oven to moderately hot 200°C (400°F/Gas 6).
3 To make the topping, cook the potatoes in a pan of boiling water until tender. Drain and mash until smooth. Place the flour and salt in a food processor and add the cheese and butter. Process in short bursts until the mixture forms crumbs. Add this mixture to the mashed potato and bring together with your hands to form a dough.
4 Roll out the dough on a floured surface, until it is 1 cm (¹/2 inch) thick. Cut into circles with a 6 cm (2¹/2 inch) diameter pastry cutter. Keep re-rolling the pastry scraps until all the dough is used. Carefully lift the circles up with your fingers, and arrange them so that they overlap on top of the cooled chicken and leek filling.
5 Brush the dough circles with the egg yolk and add a little milk if more glaze is needed. Bake for 30 minutes, or until the filling is heated through and the pastry is golden.

NUTRITION PER SERVE (6)
Protein 45 g; Fat 30 g; Carbohydrate 30 g; Dietary Fibre 4 g; Cholesterol 185 mg; 2405 kJ (570 cal)

COOK'S FILE

Note: For a lower-fat variation, you can use a non-stick frying pan to cook the chicken in Step 1. You can also replace the mature Cheddar with low-fat Cheddar and reduce the amount of butter used in the filling.

Rinse the leeks thoroughly before cooking and slice very thinly.

Remove the pan from the heat and stir in the chicken stock and cream.

Add the mustard and peppercorns to the simmering chicken and leek mixture.

Bring together the crumb mixture and mashed potato with your hands.

Roll out the dough and cut circles from it with a pastry cutter.

Arrange the circles, overlapping, on top of the cooled filling mixture.

STEAK AND KIDNEY PIE

Preparation time: 1 hour 10 minutes
  + 30 minutes refrigeration
Total cooking time: 2½–3 hours
Serves 6

1 kg (2 lb) chuck steak, trimmed
250 g (8 oz) lambs' kidneys
1 large onion, chopped
2 tablespoons oil
2 cloves garlic, crushed
2 tablespoons plain flour
1 cup (250 ml/8 fl oz) beef
  stock
1 teaspoon dried thyme
2 teaspoons soft brown sugar

Parsnip Pastry
200 g (6½ oz) parsnips, chopped
  and cooked until soft
2 cups (250 g/8 oz) self-raising
  flour
1 teaspoon ground coriander
150 g (5 oz) cold butter,
  chopped

1 egg yolk, lightly beaten

1 Cut the steak into cubes. Core and quarter the kidneys. Cook the onion in 1 tablespoon of oil until soft. Add the garlic and cook for 1 minute. Remove the onion and garlic from the pan.
2 Brown the steak and kidney in batches in the remaining oil. Add the flour and cook for 1 minute.
3 Return the onion to the pan, add the stock, thyme and sugar and mix. Bring to the boil, reduce the heat and simmer, covered, for 1½–2 hours, or until the meat is tender. For the last 15 minutes, uncover and stir to thicken. Add ½ cup (125 ml/4 fl oz) of water if too dry. Allow to cool.

4 To make the parsnip pastry, purée the parsnips in a food processor and transfer to a bowl. Process the flour, coriander and butter until crumbly. Add the parsnip and egg yolk. Process in short bursts until the mixture comes together. Turn out onto a floured surface and gather into a ball. Cover with plastic wrap and refrigerate for at least 30 minutes.
5 Preheat the oven to moderately hot 200°C (400°F/Gas 6). Divide the pastry in half. Roll out one half to line a 23 cm (9 inch) pie dish. Press well into

the sides. Fill with the steak and kidney filling. Roll out the other piece to cover the dish. Dampen the edges with water and press together to seal. Trim the excess pastry and use to decorate the top of the pie.
6 Cut 2 slits in the top, then brush with the combined egg yolk and 1 tablespoon of milk. Bake for 30 minutes, or until golden.

NUTRITION PER SERVE
Protein 50 g; Fat 35 g; Carbohydrate 40 g; Dietary Fibre 3 g; Cholesterol 345 mg; 2800 kJ (665 cal)

Remove the cores from the kidneys with a sharp knife and cut into quarters.

Remove the lid to allow the sauce to reduce down until it is very thick.

Trim away the overhanging pastry from the edge of the pie.

CHEESE AND HERB PASTRY HATS

Preparation time: 25 minutes
 + 20 minutes refrigeration
Total cooking time: 20 minutes
Makes 12

Cheese and Herb Filling
125 g (4 oz) ricotta cheese
3/4 cup (100 g/3 1/2 oz) grated Emmenthal or Gruyère cheese
2 spring onions, chopped
1 egg, lightly beaten

1/3 cup (20 g/3/4 oz) chopped herbs, such as parsley, chives or oregano

6 sheets ready-rolled puff pastry
1 egg yolk, to glaze

1 To make the cheese and herb filling, combine the cheeses, spring onion and egg in a bowl. Season with ground black pepper; add the herbs.

2 Grease a large baking tray. Cut two 12 cm (4 3/4 inch) circles from each sheet of pastry. Place 1 heaped tablespoon of filling in the centre of each, leaving a wide border. Brush the edges with a little water and form each pastry into an even 3-cornered hat shape. Pinch the edges to seal. Place on a baking tray, leaving room for them to spread.

3 Cover and refrigerate the pastries for at least 20 minutes. Preheat the oven to moderately hot 200°C (400°F/Gas 6). Mix the egg yolk with 1 teaspoon of water. Glaze the pastries, and bake for 15–20 minutes, or until puffed and golden.

NUTRITION PER PASTRY HAT
Protein 9 g; Fat 25 g; Carbohydrate 30 g; Dietary Fibre 1 g; Cholesterol 65 mg; 1545 kJ (365 cal)

Combine the cheeses, spring onion and egg in a bowl.

Form the pastries into 3-cornered hat shapes and pinch the edges to seal.

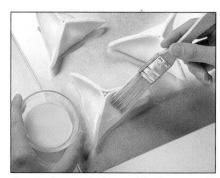

Brush the pastry hats with the egg yolk and water just before baking.

COUNTRY VEGETABLE PIES

Preparation time: 50 minutes
  + 30 minutes refrigeration
Total cooking time: 45 minutes
Serves 6

2 cups (250 g/8 oz) plain flour
125 g (4 oz) cold butter, chopped
2 egg yolks

Filling
2 new potatoes, cubed
350 g (11 oz) butternut
  pumpkin, cubed
100 g (3½ oz) broccoli, cut into
  small florets
100 g (3½ oz) cauliflower, cut
  into small florets
1 zucchini, grated
1 carrot, grated
3 spring onions, chopped
¾ cup (90 g/3 oz) grated
  Cheddar
½ cup (125 g/4 oz) ricotta
  cheese
½ cup (50 g/1¾ oz) grated
  Parmesan
¼ cup (15 g/½ oz) chopped
  parsley
1 egg, lightly beaten

1 Place the flour and butter in a food processor and process until the mixture is crumbly. Add the egg yolks and 3–4 tablespoons of water. Process in short bursts until the mixture just comes together, adding a little extra water if necessary. Turn out onto a floured surface and bring together into a ball. Cover with plastic wrap and refrigerate for at least 15 minutes.
2 To make the filling, steam or boil the potato and pumpkin for 10–15 minutes, or until just tender. Drain and place in a large bowl to cool. Gently fold in the broccoli, cauliflower, zucchini, carrot, spring onion, cheeses, parsley and beaten egg. Season to taste with salt and freshly ground black pepper.
3 Grease six 10 cm (4 inch) pie tins. Divide the pastry into 6 pieces. Roll each into a rough 20 cm (8 inch) circle. Place the pastry into the tins, leaving the excess overhanging.

4 Divide the filling between the tins. Fold over the overhanging pastry, folding or pleating as you go. Place on a baking tray. Cover and refrigerate for 15 minutes. Preheat the oven to moderately hot 190°C (375°F/Gas 4). Bake for 25–30 minutes, or until the pastry is cooked and golden brown. Serve hot.

NUTRITION PER SERVE
Protein 20 g; Fat 30 g; Carbohydrate 45 g; Dietary Fibre 6 g; Cholesterol 175 mg; 2230 kJ (530 cal)

Gently fold in the uncooked vegetables, cheese, parsley and beaten egg.

Fit the pastry circles into the tins, leaving the excess overhanging.

Fold the overhanging pastry back over the vegetable filling.

Wash the spinach thoroughly before using and remove the stalks.

Add the spring onion, feta, Parmesan, dill, eggs and nutmeg to the spinach.

Place some filling along one long edge of the pastry, fold in the sides and roll up.

Once the pastry has been rolled up to seal the filling, roll it into a firm coil.

SPINACH AND FETA FILO ROLL

Preparation time: 30 minutes
Total cooking time: 50 minutes
Serves 4–6

1 bunch (500 g/1 lb) English
    spinach
2 tablespoons olive oil
8 spring onions, finely chopped
375 g (12 oz) feta cheese,
    crumbled
1/4 cup (25 g/3/4 oz) freshly
    grated Parmesan
1/4 cup (15 g/1/2 oz) chopped dill
2 eggs, lightly beaten
1/2 teaspoon ground nutmeg

12 sheets filo pastry
olive oil, for brushing
ground nutmeg, for sprinkling

1 Cook the spinach in a pan of water over medium heat for 3–5 minutes, or until wilted. Drain, cool and squeeze out as much moisture as possible. Chop roughly and put in a large bowl.
2 Heat the olive oil in a pan and cook the spring onion for 2–3 minutes. Add to the spinach along with the feta, Parmesan, dill, eggs and nutmeg. Season with pepper and stir well.
3 Grease a 30 cm (12 inch) round pizza tray. Preheat the oven to moderately hot 190°C (375°F/Gas 5). Cover the filo with a damp tea towel and working with 1 sheet at a time, lightly brush 1 sheet with oil, fold in half lengthways and brush again. Place 3 tablespoons of the filling along one long edge, fold in the sides and roll up firmly. Form the roll into a coil, brush again with some oil and place on the tray. Repeat with the remaining sheets and filling. Arrange the coils in a single layer. Then sprinkle the top with the nutmeg. Bake for 40 minutes.

NUTRITION PER SERVE (6)
Protein 20 g; Fat 30 g; Carbohydrate 45 g; Dietary Fibre 6 g; Cholesterol 175 mg; 2230 kJ (530 cal)

COOK'S FILE

Note: Substitute dry cottage cheese for half the feta if you prefer a less salty flavour.

BACON AND EGG PIES

Preparation time: 30 minutes
Total cooking time: 25–30 minutes
Makes 6

1 teaspoon oil
4 spring onions, chopped
6 lean bacon rashers, chopped
1/2 cup (125 ml/4 fl oz) milk
1/4 cup (60 ml/2 fl oz) cream
2 tablespoons chopped parsley
pinch of ground nutmeg
7 eggs
10 sheets filo pastry
melted butter for brushing

1 Heat the oil in a pan and cook the spring onion and bacon for 2–3 minutes, then set aside to cool. Mix together the milk, cream, parsley, ground nutmeg and 1 egg and season to taste with salt and freshly ground black pepper.

2 Brush 1 sheet of filo pastry with the melted butter, then brush another sheet and lay it on top. Repeat until you have a stack of 5 sheets. Cut into 6 squares. Repeat with the remaining 5 sheets of pastry. Place 2 squares together at an angle to form a rough 8-pointed star, and fit into a 1-cup (250 ml/8 fl oz) capacity muffin tin. Repeat with the remaining squares.

3 Preheat the oven to moderately hot 200°C (400°F/Gas 6). Divide the spring onion and bacon mixture evenly between the filo pastry cups. Then pour over the egg and cream mixture and carefully break an egg on the top of the pie. Bake for 10 minutes, then reduce the oven to moderate 180°C (350°F/Gas 4) and bake for a further 10–15 minutes, or until the pastry is lightly crisp and golden and the egg is just set. Serve immediately.

NUTRITION PER SERVE
Protein 15 g; Fat 15 g; Carbohydrate 10 g; Dietary Fibre 1 g; Cholesterol 245 mg; 1130 kJ (270 cal)

Season the egg, milk, cream, parsley and nutmeg mixture.

Make an 8-pointed star with 2 pastry squares and place in the muffin tin.

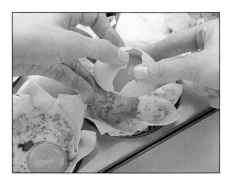

Carefully break an egg over the filling inside the pastry shell.

FETA AND PINE NUT CHEESE STRUDEL

Preparation time: 20 minutes
Total cooking time: 35 minutes
Serves 4–6

1/2 cup (80 g/2³/4 oz) pine nuts, toasted
1³/4 cups (260 g/8 oz) feta cheese, crumbled
250 g (8 oz) ricotta cheese
2 tablespoons chopped basil
4 spring onions, chopped

2 eggs, lightly beaten
9 sheets filo pastry
40 g (1¹/4 oz) butter
2 tablespoons olive oil
2–3 teaspoons sesame seeds

1 Preheat the oven to moderate 180°C (350°F/Gas 4). Mix together the pine nuts, feta, ricotta, basil, spring onion and eggs. Season with freshly ground black pepper. Brush each sheet of filo with the combined melted butter and oil and stack them one on top of the other.
2 Spread the cheese filling in the centre, covering an area of about 10 x 30 cm (4 x 12 inches). Fold in the sides of the pastry, then tuck in the ends. Carefully turn the strudel over and place on a baking tray, seam-side-down. Lightly brush the top with a little melted butter and sprinkle with the sesame seeds. Bake for 35 minutes, or until the pastry is crisp and golden. Serve warm with relish or chutney.

NUTRITION PER SERVE (6)
Protein 20 g; Fat 40 g; Carbohydrate 15 g; Dietary Fibre 1 g; Cholesterol 125 mg; 1940 kJ (460 cal)

Mix together the pine nuts, feta, ricotta, basil, spring onion and eggs.

Fold in the ends of the pastry, then each side, to enclose the filling.

Sprinkle the finished strudel with sesame seeds before baking.

PICNIC PIE WITH ROCKET PESTO

Preparation time: 1 hour
  + 40 minutes refrigeration
Total cooking time: 1 hour
Serves 6–8

2¹/4 cups (280 g/9 oz) plain flour
¹/4 cup (35 g/1¹/4 oz) polenta
150 g (5 oz) cold butter, chopped
1 egg
1 egg yolk
1–2 tablespoons polenta, extra

Filling
500 g (1 lb) eggplant
¹/4 cup (60 ml/2 fl oz) olive oil
1 large red capsicum
1 large green capsicum
1 large yellow capsicum
250 g (8 oz) mozzarella cheese,
  sliced
¹/4 cup (40 g/1¹/4 oz) sun-dried
  tomatoes, drained and sliced
1 egg yolk, lightly beaten

Rocket Pesto
1¹/2 cups (70 g/2¹/4 oz) roughly
  chopped rocket leaves
¹/4 cup (40 g/1¹/4 oz) pine nuts
2 cloves garlic, crushed
¹/2 cup (125 ml/4 fl oz) olive oil
¹/2 cup (50 g/1³/4 oz) freshly
  grated Parmesan

1 Place the flour, polenta, butter, a pinch of salt and some freshly ground black pepper into a food processor. Process until the mixture is crumbly. Add the egg, egg yolk and about 3 tablespoons of water. Process in short bursts until the mixture just comes together. Add a little extra water if necessary. Turn out onto a floured surface and gather into a ball. Cover with plastic wrap and refrigerate for at least 30 minutes. Preheat the oven to moderately hot 200°C (400°F/Gas 6). Grease a 20 cm (8 inch) springform tin and sprinkle with a little of the extra polenta.

2 Roll out two-thirds of the pastry to line the base and sides of the tin up to 0.5 cm (¹/4 inch) from the top. If the pastry breaks, patch it up with scraps. Evenly trim the edges. Refrigerate for 10 minutes. Prick with a fork and bake for 10 minutes, or until lightly browned and dry. Cool.

3 To make the filling, thickly slice the eggplant. Brush with oil and grill until browned on both sides. Quarter the capsicums and grill, skin-side-up, until the skin is black and blistered. Put in a plastic bag to cool, then peel away the skin.

4 Place alternate layers of eggplant, capsicum and cheese in the pastry case. Season well and sprinkle with the sun-dried tomatoes.

5 Roll out the remaining pastry. Brush the top edge of the pastry case with some egg yolk, place the pastry lid over and press the edges firmly. Press with a spoon or fork. Decorate with pastry shapes. Brush with the remaining egg yolk and add the remaining polenta. Bake for 40 minutes, or until lightly browned. Cool in the tin before cutting.

6 To make the rocket pesto, put the rocket, nuts and garlic in a food processer, add the oil and process until smooth. Add the cheese and process briefly. Serve cold wedges of pie with a tablespoon of pesto each.

NUTRITION PER SERVE (8)
Protein 20 g; Fat 55 g; Carbohydrate 40 g; Dietary Fibre 4 g; Cholesterol 140 mg; 2955 kJ (705 cal)

Place the flour, polenta, butter, salt and black pepper in the food processor.

Grease the springform tin and sprinkle with a little extra polenta.

Fill the pastry case with alternate layers starting with the eggplant.

Roll out the remaining third of pastry to make the pie lid.

Roll out any scraps of pastry and cut decorative shapes for the top of the pie.

Place the rocket, pine nuts and garlic for the pesto in the processor and add oil.

KANGAROO PIES

Preparation time: 30 minutes
+ 20 minutes refrigeration
Total cooking time: 1 hour 40 minutes
Serves 4

30 g (1 oz) butter
500 g (1 lb) kangaroo rump,
    cubed
2 rashers bacon, chopped
2 tablespoons plain flour
1 onion, chopped
2 carrots, chopped
2 sticks celery, chopped
100 g (3¹/2 oz) mushrooms,
    chopped
¹/3 cup (50 g/1³/4 oz) peas
1 cup (250 ml/8 fl oz) beef stock
1 tablespoon tomato paste

4 sheets ready-rolled puff
    pastry
1 egg yolk, lightly beaten, to
    glaze

1 Heat the butter in a pan and cook the kangaroo and bacon, stirring, for 2 minutes, or until the meat changes colour. Add the flour and cook for 2–3 minutes, stirring, or until the flour has thickened slightly. Add the onion, carrot, celery, mushrooms, peas, stock and tomato paste. Reduce the heat and simmer for 1 hour, stirring frequently. Season to taste and set aside to cool.
2 Grease four 12.5 cm (4³/4 inch) round pie tins. From each sheet of pastry, cut one 14 cm (5¹/2 inch) diameter circle and one 12.5 cm (4³/4 inch) diameter circle. Roll the larger circles to 16 cm (6¹/2 inch) diameter and fit into the tins. Trim any excess pastry. Spoon a quarter of the meat mixture into each. Mix the

egg yolk with 1 teaspoon of water and brush the rims. Use the smaller circles to make the lids. Press the edges to seal and decorate with the prongs of a fork. Use any pastry scraps to decorate the pie tops and make a few slits to allow steam to escape.
3 Place the pies on an oven tray; cover and refrigerate for at least 20 minutes. Preheat the oven to moderately hot 200°C (400°F/Gas 6). Brush the pastry with the egg yolk and water. Bake for

10 minutes, reduce the temperature to moderate 180°C (350°F/Gas 4) and bake for a further 20 minutes, or until puffed and golden brown.

NUTRITION PER SERVE
Protein 50 g; Fat 50 g; Carbohydrate 70 g; Dietary Fibre 7 g; Cholesterol 185 mg; 4060 kJ (965 cal)

COOK'S FILE

Variation: You can replace kangaroo meat with beef.

Add the chopped onion, carrot, celery and mushrooms to the pan.

Roll out the larger circles so that they will line the tins.

Fit the smaller circles of pastry over the filling and seal the edges.

MEXICAN CHILLI PIES

Preparation time: 1 hour
 + 15 minutes refrigeration
Total cooking time: 1 hour 25 minutes
Serves 6

1 tablespoon oil
1 onion, chopped
2 cloves garlic, crushed
2 teaspoons ground cumin
1 teaspoon ground coriander
1/2 teaspoon chilli powder
1/2 teaspoon paprika
2 carrots, chopped
1 red capsicum, chopped
425 g (14 oz) can red kidney
    beans, drained
425 g (14 oz) can chopped
    tomatoes
1 cup (125 g/4 oz) grated
    Cheddar
sliced avocado, sour cream and
    paprika, to serve

2 cups (250 g/8 oz) plain flour
125 g (4 oz) cold butter,
    chopped
1 cup (125 g/4 oz) grated
    Cheddar, extra

1 Heat the oil in a heavy-based pan and cook the onion until softened. Add the garlic and spices; cook for 1 minute. Add the carrot and capsicum and toss to coat with the spices. Stir in the kidney beans and tomatoes. Bring to the boil, then reduce the heat and simmer, stirring occasionally, for 50 minutes, or until the liquid has been absorbed.
2 To make the pastry, process the flour, butter and cheese in a food processor until crumbly. Add 1–2 tablespoons of iced water and

process in short bursts until the mixture just comes together. Turn out onto a floured surface and quickly gather into a ball. Cover with plastic wrap and refrigerate for at least 15 minutes. Preheat the oven to moderately hot 200°C (400°F/Gas 6).
3 Grease 6 shallow 11 cm (4¹/2 inch) flan tins. Divide the pastry into 6 pieces. Roll each into a 14 cm (5¹/2 inch) circle on a sheet of baking paper, and line the tins. Cover with baking paper and fill evenly with

baking beads or rice. Bake for 8 minutes. Remove the paper and beads and bake for a further 8 minutes. Allow to cool.
4 Add the filling to the pastry shells. Top with the Cheddar and bake for 10 minutes, or until the cheese has melted. Add the avocado, a spoonful of sour cream and some paprika.

NUTRITION PER SERVE
Protein 20 g; Fat 40 g; Carbohydrate 50 g; Dietary Fibre 10 g; Cholesterol 110 mg; 2745 kJ (655 cal)

Stir the mixture well to coat the carrot and capsicum in the spices.

Use some melted butter to grease all the flan tins.

Line the pastry bases with baking paper and fill with baking beads or rice.

CHICKEN AND BACON GOUGERE

Preparation time: 40 minutes
Total cooking time: 50 minutes
Serves 6

60 g (2 oz) butter
1–2 cloves garlic, crushed
1 red onion, chopped
3 rashers bacon, chopped
1/4 cup (30 g/1 oz) plain flour
1 1/2 cups (375 ml/12 fl oz) milk
1/2 cup (125 ml/4 fl oz) cream
2 teaspoons wholegrain mustard
250 g (8 oz) cooked chicken
1/2 cup (30 g/1 oz) chopped
   parsley

Choux Pastry
60 g (2 oz) butter, chopped
1/2 cup (60 g/2 oz) plain flour
2 eggs, lightly beaten
35 g (1 1/4 oz) grated Parmesan

1 Melt the butter in a frying pan and cook the garlic, onion and bacon for 5–7 minutes, stirring occasionally, until cooked but not browned. Stir in the flour and cook for 1 minute. Gradually add the milk and stir until thickened. Simmer for 2 minutes then add the cream and mustard. Remove from the heat and fold in the chopped chicken and parsley. Add pepper.
2 To make the choux pastry, place the butter and 1/2 cup (125 ml/4 fl oz) of water in a pan and stir until melted, then bring to the boil. Beat in the flour for 2 minutes, or until the mixture leaves the sides of the pan. Cool for 5 minutes. Gradually beat in the egg with an electric beater, beating well after each addition, until thick and glossy. Add the Parmesan.
3 Preheat the oven to hot 210°C (415°F/Gas 6–7). Grease a deep 23 cm (9 inch) ovenproof dish, pour in the filling and spoon heaped tablespoons of choux around the outside. Bake for 10 minutes, then reduce the oven to moderate 180°C (350°F/Gas 4) and bake for 20 minutes, or until the choux is puffed and golden. Sprinkle with a little more grated Parmesan.

NUTRITION PER SERVE
Protein 25 g; Fat 35 g; Carbohydrate 15 g; Dietary Fibre 1 g; Cholesterol 215 mg; 2010 kJ (480 cal)

Stir the garlic, onion and bacon until cooked but not browned.

Bring the butter and water to the boil, then add the flour all at once.

Beat with a wooden spoon until the choux leaves the side of the pan.

Pour the filling into the ovenproof dish then spoon the choux around the outside.

CHARGRILLED VEGETABLE PIE WITH POLENTA PASTRY

Preparation time: 1 hour
+ 50 minutes refrigeration
Total cooking time: 55 minutes
Serves 4–6

Polenta Pastry
1 cup (125 g/4 oz) plain flour
1/2 cup (75 g/21/2 oz) polenta
90 g (3 oz) butter, cubed
90 g (3 oz) cream cheese, cubed

1 kg (2 lb) eggplant, sliced
  lengthways
2 large tablespoons olive oil
1–2 cloves garlic, crushed
2 red capsicums, halved and
  seeded
8 cherry tomatoes, halved
handful of small basil leaves
2 teaspoons baby capers
1 teaspoon balsamic vinegar
1 teaspoon olive oil, extra

1 Place the flour, polenta, butter and cream cheese in a food processor. Process in short bursts until the mixture just comes together. Add 1–2 teaspoons of cold water if needed. Turn out onto a floured surface and quickly bring together into a ball. Cover with plastic wrap and refrigerate for at least 30 minutes.
2 Brush the eggplant with the combined olive oil and garlic and grill for 10–12 minutes, turning once and brushing 2–3 times during cooking. Grill the capsicum, skin-side-up, for 5–8 minutes, until the skin has blackened. Cool in a plastic bag, remove the skin and slice. Grill the tomatoes, cut-side-up, for 2–3 minutes.

3 Roll out the pastry on baking paper to fit a shallow 21 x 28 cm (81/2 x 11 inch) loose-based flan tin. Press well into the sides and trim off any excess. Refrigerate for 20 minutes. Preheat the oven to moderately hot 190°C (375°F/Gas 5). Cover the pastry shell with baking paper and fill evenly with baking beads. Bake for 15 minutes. Remove the paper and beads and bake for 15 minutes, or until cooked.
4 Layer the pastry with capsicum, eggplant, tomato halves, some basil leaves and capers. Brush with the combined balsamic vinegar and oil.

NUTRITION PER SERVE (6)
Protein 7 g; Fat 25 g; Carbohydrate 30 g; Dietary Fibre 6 g; Cholesterol 55 mg; 1600 kJ (380 cal)

Crush the garlic; halve and seed the capsicums and halve the cherry tomatoes.

Process the mixture in short bursts until it just comes together.

Roll out the pastry on a sheet of baking paper.

CHICKEN AND WATERCRESS STRUDEL

Preparation time: 30 minutes
Total cooking time: 50 minutes
Serves 6

3/4 cup (60 g/2 oz) fresh white breadcrumbs
1–2 teaspoons sesame seeds
1 bunch (60 g/2 oz) watercress
4 chicken breast fillets
25 g (3/4 oz) butter
3 tablespoons Dijon mustard
1 cup (250 ml/8 fl oz) thick cream

15 sheets filo pastry
100 g (3 1/2 oz) butter, melted

1 Preheat the oven to moderately hot 190°C (375°F/Gas 5) and bake the breadcrumbs and sesame seeds, on separate trays, until golden. Steam the watercress for 3–5 minutes, until just wilted, and squeeze out any water.

2 Slice the chicken into thin strips. Heat the butter in a pan and stir-fry the chicken until just cooked. Remove from the pan and season to taste. Stir the mustard and cream into the pan and simmer gently until reduced to about 1/2 cup (125 ml/4 fl oz). Remove from the heat and stir in the chicken and watercress.

3 Brush a sheet of filo with melted butter and sprinkle with toasted breadcrumbs. Lay another filo sheet on top, brush with butter and sprinkle with breadcrumbs. Repeat with the remaining filo and breadcrumbs and place on a baking tray.

4 Place the chicken filling along the centre of the pastry. Fold the sides over and roll into a parcel, with the join underneath. Brush with the remaining butter and add the sesame seeds. Bake for 30 minutes, or until golden. Cool slightly before serving.

NUTRITION PER SERVE
Protein 25 g; Fat 65 g; Carbohydrate 30 g; Dietary Fibre 2 g; Cholesterol 235 mg; 3350 kJ (795 cal)

Steam the watercress until lightly cooked, then drain and squeeze out the water.

Layer the buttered sheets of filo pastry and place on a baking tray.

Fold in the pastry sides to enclose the filling, then roll up into a parcel.

68

INDIAN DHAL PIES

Preparation time: 45 minutes
Total cooking time: 1 hour 15 minutes
Serves 6

300 g (10 oz) potato, diced
450 g (14 oz) butternut
    pumpkin, diced
2 carrots, chopped
2 tablespoons olive oil
60 g (2 oz) broccoli florets
1 onion, chopped
1 teaspoon ground turmeric
1 teaspoon garam masala
1 teaspoon ground cumin
2 cloves garlic, crushed
1 teaspoon black mustard seeds
1/2 cup (125 g/4 oz) red lentils
2/3 cup (85 g/3 oz) grated
    Cheddar
1/4 cup (60 g/2 oz) thick yoghurt

2 cups (220 g/7 oz) besan flour
1/3 cup (35 g/1 1/4 oz) skim milk
    powder
125 g (4 oz) cold butter, diced
1 egg, lightly beaten

1 Preheat the oven to 200°C (400°F/ Gas 6). Place the potato, pumpkin and carrot in a baking dish and drizzle with the oil. Bake for 40 minutes, turning once, until golden brown. Steam the broccoli for 3–5 minutes.

2 Cook the onion in a little oil until soft. Add the spices, garlic and mustard seeds and cook for 1 minute. Add the lentils and 1 cup (250 ml/ 8 fl oz) of water. Bring to the boil then simmer, stirring, for 25–30 minutes, or until the liquid is absorbed and the lentils are soft.

3 Grease six 10.5 cm (4 1/4 inch) fluted loose-based flan tins. Process the flour, skim milk powder and butter for 15 seconds until crumbly. Add the egg and 1 tablespoon of water and process in short bursts until the mixture comes together. Turn out, gather into a ball and roll out to line the tins. Cover with baking paper and baking beads and bake for 7 minutes. Remove the paper and beads and bake for a further 5 minutes. Allow to cool.

4 Divide the lentil dhal among the pastry shells, top with the roast vegetables, broccoli and Cheddar. Bake the pies for 5 minutes to melt the cheese and top with a little plain thick yoghurt, to serve.

NUTRITION PER SERVE
Protein 20 g; Fat 35 g; Carbohydrate 40 g; Dietary Fibre 11 g; Cholesterol 100 mg; 2255 kJ (535 cal)

Cut the butternut pumpkin and potato into small cubes and slice the carrots.

Add the lentils to the pan and stir them to coat thoroughly with the spices.

Simmer the dhal mixture until the lentils are soft and all the liquid has gone.

69

TANDOORI LAMB PIE

Preparation time: 45 minutes
+ 20 minutes refrigeration
Total cooking time: 1 hour 30 minutes
Serves 4–6

1 cup (125 g/4 oz) plain flour
60 g (2 oz) cold butter, cubed
2 teaspoons coriander seeds
2 teaspoons cumin seeds
2 teaspoons poppy seeds
1 egg yolk

Filling
850 g (1 lb 11 oz) boned lamb
    shoulder
2 tablespoons oil
2 onions, chopped
1 clove garlic, crushed
2 teaspoons grated fresh ginger
1 teaspoon chilli powder
2 teaspoons garam masala
1 teaspoon ground cumin
1/2 teaspoon ground turmeric
2 carrots, chopped
1 1/4 cups (315 ml/10 fl oz) beef
    stock
1 tablespoon plain flour
1 teaspoon sugar
2 tablespoons lemon juice
200 g (6 1/2 oz) yoghurt
1 egg yolk, lightly beaten, to
    glaze

1 To make the pastry, process the flour and butter in a food processor until the mixture is crumbly. Season with a pinch of salt. Add the coriander, cumin and poppy seeds and process until combined. Then add the egg yolk and 2 tablespoons of water. Process in short bursts until the mixture just comes together, adding a little extra water if necessary. Turn out onto a floured surface and quickly bring together into a ball. Cover with plastic wrap and refrigerate for at least 20 minutes.

2 To make the filling, trim any excess fat from the lamb and cut into large cubes. Heat the oil in a pan and brown the lamb in batches. Add the onion and cook until translucent. Add the garlic, ginger and spices and stir over the heat for about 1 minute, or until aromatic. Stir in the carrot and stock. Bring to the boil, reduce the heat and simmer, covered, for 50 minutes, or until the lamb is tender. Remove from the heat. Mix together the flour and 2 tablespoons of water, until smooth. Stir into the meat, return to the heat and then stir until the mixture boils and thickens. Add the sugar, lemon juice and yoghurt and stir until well combined. Season with a good pinch of salt, if you want.

3 Spoon the mixture into a deep 20 cm (8 inch) square or round pie dish and allow to cool. Preheat the oven to moderately hot 200°C (400°F/Gas 6).

4 Roll out the pastry on a sheet of baking paper until it is large enough to cover the pie dish. Place the pastry over the filling and pinch the edges decoratively with your fingers. Then brush with the lightly beaten egg yolk and bake for 25–30 minutes, or until the pastry is browned and crisp.

NUTRITION PER SERVE (6)
Protein 40 g; Fat 25 g; Carbohydrate 25 g; Dietary Fibre 3 g; Cholesterol 185 mg; 1920 kJ (455 cal)

COOK'S FILE

Note: If you want, you can prepare the pie ahead and store, covered, in the refrigerator for up to 1 day before baking.

Add the coriander, cumin and poppy seeds to the food processor.

Brown the lamb in batches, returning all the meat to the pan.

Stir the chopped carrot and beef stock into the lamb mixture.

Add the sugar, lemon juice and yoghurt to the pan and stir well.

Roll out the pastry until it is large enough to cover the pie dish.

Cover the filling with the pastry and pinch the edges for a decorative finish.

CHILLI CHICKEN PIE

Preparation time: 45 minutes
Total cooking time: 1 hour 20 minutes
Serves 4–6

2 tablespoons olive oil
1 onion, chopped
750 g (1¹/₂ lb) chicken breast
    fillets, cut into chunks
3 cloves garlic, crushed
1 teaspoon chilli powder
2 teaspoons cumin seeds
1 tablespoon plain flour
2 x 410 g (13 oz) cans chopped
    tomatoes
1 tablespoon soft brown sugar

1 red capsicum, thinly sliced
375 g (12 oz) can red kidney
    beans, rinsed and drained
15 sheets filo pastry
100 g (3¹/₂ oz) butter, melted

1 Heat half the oil in a large frying pan and cook the onion until softened and golden. Remove from the pan, add the remaining oil and brown the chicken over high heat.

2 Stir in the garlic, chilli powder and cumin seeds and cook for 1 minute. Return the onion to the pan, stir in the flour and cook for 30 seconds. Stir in the chopped tomatoes.

3 Add the sugar and capsicum and simmer over low heat for 40 minutes,

until reduced and thickened. Increase the heat and, stirring continuously to prevent burning, add the kidney beans. Allow to cool, then spoon into a casserole dish. Preheat the oven to moderate 180°C (350°F/Gas 4).

4 Cut the filo sheets in half, brush with the melted butter and scrunch up. Place on top of the filling, to cover it completely (you may not need to use all the filo pastry). Brush with the remaining butter and bake for 25–30 minutes, or until the pastry is golden and crisp.

NUTRITION PER SERVE (6)
Protein 40 g; Fat 25 g; Carbohydrate 35 g; Dietary Fibre 7 g; Cholesterol 105 mg; 2175 kJ (515 cal)

Stir the garlic, chilli powder and cumin seeds into the browned chicken.

Add the kidney beans to the filling mixture.

Scrunch up the sheets of filo pastry and arrange them on top of the filling.

STEAK AND MUSHROOM PIES

Preparation time: 40 minutes
Total cooking time: 2 hours
  + 1 hour refrigeration
Serves 4

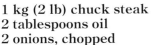

1 kg (2 lb) chuck steak
2 tablespoons oil
2 onions, chopped
250 g (8 oz) large mushrooms,
  chopped
1³/4 cups (440 ml/14 fl oz) beef
  stock
1 tablespoon soy sauce
2 bay leaves
2 juniper berries
¹/3 cup (40 g/1¹/4 oz) plain flour
¹/4 cup (15 g/¹/2 oz) chopped
  parsley

4 sheets ready-rolled puff
  pastry
1 egg yolk, lightly beaten, to
  glaze

1 Trim the excess fat from the meat
and cut into large cubes. Heat the oil
in a large pan and cook the meat in
two batches over medium heat, until
browned. Drain on paper towels. Add
the onions to the pan and cook until
translucent. Return the meat to the
pan with the mushrooms, stock, soy
sauce, bay leaves and juniper berries.
Season with ¹/2 teaspoon of pepper.
Bring to the boil, reduce the heat and
simmer, covered, for 1¹/2 hours, or
until the meat is tender.
2 Remove the pan from the heat and
gradually stir in the combined flour
and 4 tablespoons of water. Return to
the heat and stir until the mixture
boils and thickens. Add the parsley,

remove the bay leaves and season
with salt. Cool completely. Preheat the
oven to hot 210°C (415°F/Gas 6–7).
3 Grease four 1¹/2 cup (375 ml/
12 fl oz) pie dishes. Spoon the meat
filling into the prepared dishes and
brush the rims with some egg yolk.
Cover with pastry and press the edges
to seal, then trim. Using the leftover
pastry, cut out mushroom shapes to

decorate the tops. Decorate the edges
using the back of a knife. Brush the
tops with egg yolk and using a sharp
knife, make small slits in the tops.
Bake for 20 minutes, or until the
pastry is browned.

NUTRITION PER SERVE
Protein 65 g; Fat 55 g; Carbohydrate 70 g;
Dietary Fibre 5 g; Cholesterol 255 mg;
4430 kJ (1055 cal)

*Cook the meat in batches so that it
browns rather than stews.*

*When the mixture boils and thickens add
the chopped parsley.*

*Decorate the edges of the pies using the
back of a knife.*

SESAME SPINACH PIE

Preparation time: 30 minutes
+ 15 minutes refrigeration
Total cooking time: 50 minutes
Serves 4

1½ cups (185 g/6 oz) plain flour
100 g (3½ oz) cold butter,
  chopped
1 egg, lightly beaten
1 tablespoon sesame seeds

Filling
1 bunch (500 g/1 lb) English
  spinach
1 tablespoon butter
1 small leek, chopped
2 eggs, lightly beaten
60 g (2 oz) feta cheese, crumbled
100 g (3½ oz) ricotta cheese
⅓ cup (35 g/1¼ oz) dry
  breadcrumbs
3 teaspoons chopped thyme
1 egg yolk, lightly beaten, to
  glaze

1 To make the pastry, process the flour and butter in a food processor until crumbly. Season with a pinch of salt. Add the egg and process in short bursts until the mixture just comes together. Turn out onto a floured surface and quickly bring together into a ball. Cover with plastic wrap and refrigerate for at least 15 minutes. Preheat the oven to moderately hot 200°C (400°F/Gas 6). Grease a large pizza tray or baking tray; sprinkle with half the sesame seeds.
2 To make the filling, remove any thick stems from the spinach leaves and steam or microwave the leaves until just wilted. Drain; squeeze the excess liquid and finely chop. Heat the butter in a small pan and cook the leek for 5 minutes, or until just softened. Cool. Combine with the spinach, eggs, cheeses, breadcrumbs, thyme and some freshly ground black pepper.
3 Roll out half of the pastry into a 25 cm (10 inch) circle. Place on the tray. Spoon the filling into the centre, leaving a border; then brush the edge with water. Roll out the remaining pastry into a slightly larger circle and lay over the filling, pressing the edges to seal. Using a sharp knife, trim the edges and press with a fork to seal. Brush with egg yolk and sprinkle with the remaining sesame seeds. Bake for 40 minutes, or until the pastry is browned and crisp.

NUTRITION PER SERVE
Protein 20 g; Fat 40 g; Carbohydrate 40 g; Dietary Fibre 7 g; Cholesterol 275 mg; 2490 kJ (590 cal)

Process the flour and butter until crumbly, then season with a pinch of salt.

Squeeze the excess water from the wilted spinach leaves and finely chop.

Brush the pastry border around the filling with water.

LENTIL COTTAGE PIE

Preparation time: 30 minutes
Total cooking time: 1 hour 40 minutes
Serves 6

300 g (10 oz) brown lentils
2 tablespoons olive oil
1 onion, chopped
3 sticks celery, diced
1 large carrot, diced
1 red capsicum, diced
3 cloves garlic, crushed
2¹/₂ teaspoons ground cumin
2¹/₂ teaspoons ground coriander
1 teaspoon sweet paprika
425 g (14 oz) can chopped
    tomatoes
1¹/₂ cups (375 ml/12 fl oz)
    chicken or vegetable stock
1 tablespoon tomato paste
2 teaspoons soft brown sugar
1–2 teaspoons salt

Sweet Potato Topping
1 kg (2 lb) orange sweet
    potatoes, chopped
50 g (1³/₄ oz) butter
¹/₄ cup (60 ml/2 fl oz) milk
2 tablespoons freshly grated
    Parmesan
chopped parsley, to serve

1 Cook the lentils in unsalted boiling water for 30–40 minutes, or until tender. Heat the olive oil in a large pan and cook the onion until soft and golden. Add the celery, carrot, capsicum, garlic, cumin, coriander and paprika and cook for 2 minutes, or until fragrant.
2 Drain the lentils and add to the onion mixture. Stir in the chopped tomatoes, stock, tomato paste and sugar. Simmer, covered, over low heat for 30 minutes. Uncover and simmer for a further 10 minutes. Add 1–2 tea-spoons of salt and some freshly ground black pepper. Spoon into a large casserole or pie dish. Preheat the oven to moderate 180°C (350°F/Gas 4).
3 To make the sweet potato topping, cook the potato in a pan of salted boiling water until very tender. Drain well. Mash with the butter and milk until smooth. Season to taste with salt.

4 Carefully spoon the sweet potato topping over the lentil mixture and fluff up with a fork or the back of a spoon. Bake for 20 minutes. Sprinkle with the grated Parmesan and scatter with the chopped parsley before serving.

NUTRITION PER SERVE
Protein 20 g; Fat 15 g; Carbohydrate 50 g; Dietary Fibre 15 g; Cholesterol 25 mg; 1750 kJ (415 cal)

Finely dice the sticks of celery, large carrot and capsicum.

Add the drained lentils to the pan with the onion mixture.

Spoon the sweet potato topping over the lentil filling and fluff with a fork.

BABY VEGETABLES IN FILO BASKETS

Preparation time: 50 minutes
Total cooking time: 25 minutes
Serves 2

Filo Baskets
8 sheets filo pastry
2–3 tablespoons olive oil
2 tablespoons sesame seeds

Filling
1 bunch (155 g/5 oz) asparagus, sliced diagonally
8 baby corn, halved
125 g (4 oz) baby carrots, trimmed and halved
70 g (2¼ oz) broccoli florets
100 g (3½ oz) baby zucchini, trimmed
8 baby capsicums, halved
60 g (2 oz) snow peas
2 egg yolks
1 tablespoon white wine vinegar
120 g (4 oz) butter, melted
1 tablespoon lemon juice
1 tablespoon chopped chives

1 Preheat the oven to moderate 180°C (350°F/Gas 4). Grease 4 small oven-proof dishes, and brush the outsides with some of the olive oil. Place upturned, on a greased baking tray.
2 Take 2 sheets of the filo pastry and lay them out separately. Brush with olive oil and sprinkle with ¾ teaspoon of sesame seeds. Take another 2 sheets of filo pastry and lay one over each of the other two oiled sheets. Brush with olive oil and sprinkle with some sesame seeds. Repeat until you have 2 stacks of filo pastry, each with 4 sheets interleaved with sesame seeds.

3 Cut out a 20 cm (8 inch) circle from each pastry stack (use a bowl as a guide). Carefully mould the stacks around the upturned dishes so that they will form a basket shape when removed. Bake for 15 minutes, or until golden and cooked. Remove from the oven and carefully lift the filo baskets off the dishes and onto warmed serving plates.
4 Steam or microwave all the vegetables until they are tender, then set aside and keep them warm.
5 Place the egg yolks in a food processor and add the vinegar. Process for a few seconds then, with the motor running, slowly add the hot melted butter in a thin stream. The heat of the butter will cause the egg yolks and vinegar to thicken. Finally add the lemon juice. Season with salt and white pepper to taste.
6 Fill each filo basket with an assortment of the baby vegetables; drizzle with the sauce and scatter with chives, to serve.

NUTRITION PER SERVE
Protein 20 g; Fat 90 g; Carbohydrate 50 g; Dietary Fibre 12 g; Cholesterol 330 mg; 4460 kJ (1060 cal)

COOK'S FILE

Hint: To prevent the filo pastry from sticking to the dish, cover each dish tightly with foil. Oil the foil and allow the dishes to cool before removing the pastries from each one. Carefully lift each pastry from its dish and then peel away the foil before serving.

When you are microwaving vegetables, place in a microwave-safe dish and arrange according to size with the larger vegetables—such as the broccoli florets—around the edge of the dish and the smaller vegetables—such as the snow peas—in the centre.

Prepare the different vegetables for steaming or microwaving.

Brush 2 filo sheets with olive oil and sprinkle with some sesame seeds.

Cut a 20 cm (8 inch) circle from each pastry stack, using a bowl as a guide.

Carefully mould the pastry circles around the upturned dishes.

Steam or microwave all the vegetables until they are tender.

Slowly add the hot melted butter to the food processor in a thin stream.

77

FREEFORM PRAWN PIES

Preparation time: 30 minutes
 + 15 minutes refrigeration
Total cooking time: 30 minutes
Serves 4

2 cups (250 g/8 oz) plain flour
125 g (4 oz) cold butter, cubed

1 tablespoon peanut oil
5 cm (2 inch) piece fresh ginger,
  grated
3 cloves garlic, crushed
1 kg (2 lb) peeled raw prawns,
  deveined
1/3 cup (80 ml/2³/4 fl oz) sweet
  chilli sauce
1/3 cup (80 ml/2³/4 fl oz) lime
  juice
1/3 cup (80 ml/2³/4 fl oz) thick
  cream
1/2 cup (25 g/³/4 oz) chopped
  coriander leaves
1 egg yolk, lightly beaten,
  to glaze

1 Process the flour and butter in a food processor until crumbly. Add 3 tablespoons of water. Process in short bursts until the mixture just comes together. Add a little extra water if needed. Turn onto a floured surface and quickly bring together into a ball. Cover with plastic wrap and refrigerate for at least 15 minutes.
2 Preheat the oven to moderately hot 200°C (400°F/Gas 6). Heat the oil in a large frying pan or wok and stir-fry the ginger, garlic and prawns for 2–3 minutes. Remove the prawns and set aside. Add the chilli sauce, lime juice and cream and simmer over medium heat, until the sauce has reduced by about one third. Return the prawns to the pan and add the coriander leaves.

3 Grease 2 baking trays. Divide the pastry into 4 and roll out each piece on a sheet of baking paper into a 20 cm (8 inch) circle. Divide the filling between each circle and fold over the edges. Brush the pastry with the egg yolk. Bake for 25 minutes. Serve immediately, garnished with lime zest.

NUTRITION PER SERVE
Protein 60 g; Fat 40 g; Carbohydrate 55 g; Dietary Fibre 3 g; Cholesterol 520 mg; 3470 kJ (825 cal)

Stir-fry the ginger, garlic and prawns until the prawns have turned pink.

Simmer the sauce over medium heat until it has reduced by one third.

Fold the edges of the pastry circles over the prawn filling.

HAM, CHEESE AND SPINACH FILO PIES

Preparation time: 30 minutes
Total cooking time: 25 minutes
Serves 4

1 kg (2 lb) English spinach
10 sheets filo pastry
60 g (2 oz) butter, melted
16 slices smoked ham
16 slices Swiss cheese
1 teaspoon poppy seeds

1 Preheat the oven to moderately hot 200°C (400°F/Gas 6). Rinse the spinach, then place in a pan with just the water clinging to the leaves, cover and heat until wilted. Cool and squeeze out the excess water. Spread out on a tray and set aside to dry.
2 Cover the filo sheets with a damp tea towel to prevent them drying out. Brush 1 sheet of pastry with melted butter. Brush another sheet and place on top. Repeat with 3 more sheets. Cut the stack in half. Place 2 slices of ham in the centre of each and top with

some spinach and 2 slices of cheese. Repeat these layers once more. Repeat the whole process with the remaining pastry, ham, spinach and cheese.
3 Fold over the sides and ends of the pastries to make 4 parcels. Place on 2 greased baking trays; brush with the remaining butter and sprinkle with the poppy seeds. Bake for 20–25 minutes, or until golden brown.

NUTRITION PER SERVE
Protein 50 g; Fat 40 g; Carbohydrate 20 g; Dietary Fibre 7 g; Cholesterol 150 mg; 2615 kJ (620 cal)

Spread out the wilted spinach leaves on a tray to dry.

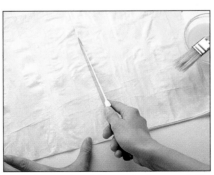
Cut the stack of layered sheets of filo pastry in half.

Repeat the layers of ham, spinach leaves and Swiss cheese.

TARTS

ITALIAN SUMMER TART

Preparation time: 40 minutes
  + 50 minutes refrigeration
Total cooking time: 1 hour
Serves 4–6

1¹/2 cups (185 g/6 oz) plain flour
90 g (3 oz) cold butter, chopped
1 egg yolk

Filling
1 tablespoon olive oil
2 small red onions, sliced
1 tablespoon balsamic vinegar
1 teaspoon soft brown sugar
1 tablespoon thyme leaves
170 g (5¹/2 oz) jar marinated
    quartered artichokes, drained
2 slices prosciutto, cut into
    strips
12 black olives
thyme leaves, to garnish

1 Place the flour and butter in a food processor and process for 15 seconds, or until the mixture resembles fine breadcrumbs. Add the egg yolk and 2–3 tablespoons of water. Process in short bursts until the mixture just comes together, adding a little extra water if necessary. Turn out onto a floured surface and gather into a ball. Cover with plastic wrap and refrigerate for at least 30 minutes.
2 Roll the pastry between 2 sheets of baking paper until it is large enough to fit and overlap a 35 x 10 cm (14 x 4 inch) rectangular loose-based flan tin. Carefully lift the pastry into the tin and press it well into the sides. Trim off any excess pastry using a sharp knife or by rolling the rolling pin across the top of the tin. Cover and refrigerate for a further 20 minutes. Preheat the oven to moderately hot 190°C (375°F/Gas 5). Cover the pastry shell with baking paper and fill evenly with baking beads, rice or beans. Bake for 15 minutes. Remove the paper and beads and bake for a further 15 minutes, or until the pastry is golden and cooked. Allow to cool on a wire rack.
3 Heat the oil in a pan, add the onion slices and cook, stirring occasionally, for 15 minutes. Add the balsamic vinegar and brown sugar and cook for a further 15 minutes. Remove from the heat, stir through the thyme leaves and set aside to cool.
4 Spread the onion evenly over the base of the cooked pastry. Arrange the quartered artichoke pieces on top of the onion, then fill the spaces in-between with the rolled-up pieces of prosciutto and the black olives. Sprinkle with the extra thyme leaves and freshly ground black pepper. Serve at room temperature.

NUTRITION PER SERVE (6)
Protein 6 g; Fat 15 g; Carbohydrate 25 g; Dietary Fibre 2 g; Cholesterol 70 mg; 1155 kJ (275 cal)

Once the mixture resembles fine crumbs, add the egg yolk and a little water.

Fill the spaces in between with rolled-up pieces of prosciutto and black olives.

THAI THREE MUSHROOM TART

Preparation time: 25 minutes
Total cooking time: 1 hour 10 minutes
Serves 8

375 g (12 oz) block puff pastry
1 teaspoon sesame oil
2 teaspoons oil
150 g (5 oz) shiitake
   mushrooms, trimmed
150 g (5 oz) button mushrooms,
   halved
150 g (5 oz) oyster mushrooms,
   halved
1/2 cup (125 ml/4 fl oz) coconut
   milk
1 stalk lemon grass, chopped

1 1/2 teaspoons grated fresh
   ginger
1 clove garlic, chopped
2 tablespoons chopped
   coriander leaves and stems
1 egg
1 tablespoon plain flour
1 spring onion, sliced diagonally

1 Preheat the oven to hot 210°C (415°F/Gas 6–7). Grease a shallow 19 cm x 28 cm (7 1/2 x 11 inch) rectangular loose-based flan tin, or a 25 cm (10 inch) round loose-based flan tin. Roll out the pastry to line the base and sides of the tin and trim off any excess. Prick all over using a fork. Bake for 20 minutes, or until crisp, then cool. While cooling, gently press down the pastry if it has puffed too

high. Reduce the oven to moderately hot 200°C (400°F/Gas 6).
2 Heat the oils in a pan, add the shiitake and button mushrooms and stir until lightly browned. Add the oyster mushrooms, then cool. Pour away any liquid.
3 Process the coconut milk, lemon grass, ginger, garlic and coriander until fairly smooth. Add the egg and flour and blend in short bursts until combined. Season to taste.
4 Pour the mixture into the pastry, add the mushrooms and then the spring onion. Bake for 30 minutes, or until set.

NUTRITION PER SERVE
Protein 5 g; Fat 15 g; Carbohydrate 20 g; Dietary Fibre 2 g; Cholesterol 35 mg; 1045 kJ (250 cal)

Trim the shiitake mushrooms and halve the oyster and button mushrooms.

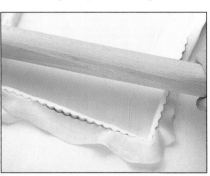

Trim the excess pastry quickly and easily by running a rolling pin over the tin.

Add the egg and flour to the coconut milk mixture and blend in short bursts.

ROASTED TOMATO AND ZUCCHINI TARTLETS

Preparation time: 45 minutes
Total cooking time: 1 hour 20 minutes
Serves 6

3 Roma tomatoes, halved
 lengthways
1 teaspoon balsamic vinegar
1 teaspoon olive oil
3 small zucchini, sliced
375 g (12 oz) block puff pastry
1 egg yolk, beaten, to glaze
12 small black olives
24 capers, rinsed and drained

Pistachio Mint Pesto
1/2 cup (75 g/2 1/2 oz) unsalted
 shelled pistachio nuts
2 cups (40 g/1 1/4 oz) firmly
 packed mint leaves
2 cloves garlic, crushed
1/3 cup (80 ml/2 3/4 fl oz) olive oil
1/2 cup (50 g/1 3/4 oz) freshly
 grated Parmesan

1 Preheat the oven to slow 150°C (300°F/Gas 2). Place the tomatoes, cut-side-up, on a baking tray. Roast for 30 minutes, brush with the combined vinegar and oil and roast for a further 30 minutes. Increase the oven to hot 210°C (415°F/Gas 6–7).
2 To make the pesto, place the pistachios, mint and garlic in a processor and process for 15 seconds. With the motor running, slowly pour in the olive oil. Add the Parmesan and process briefly.
3 Preheat the grill and line with foil. Place the zucchini in a single layer on the foil and brush with the remaining balsamic vinegar and oil. Grill for about 5 minutes, turning once.

4 Roll the pastry out to 25 x 40 cm (10 x 16 inches) and cut out six 12 cm (4 3/4 inch) circles. Put on a greased baking tray and brush with egg yolk. Spread a tablespoon of pesto on each, leaving a 2 cm (3/4 inch) border. Divide the zucchini among the pastries and top with tomato halves. Bake for 15 minutes, or until golden. Top with olives, capers and black pepper.

NUTRITION PER SERVE
Protein 15 g; Fat 60 g; Carbohydrate 35 g; Dietary Fibre 6 g; Cholesterol 80 mg; 3040 kJ (725 cal)

Roast the tomatoes for 30 minutes, then brush with the vinegar and oil.

Add the grated Parmesan to the pesto and process briefly until well mixed.

Arrange a few grilled zucchini slices over the pesto, leaving a clear border.

SPINACH AND RICOTTA LATTICE TART

Preparation time: 50 minutes
+ 15 minutes refrigeration
Total cooking time: 50 minutes
Serves 6

2 cups (250 g/8 oz) plain flour
125 g (4 oz) cold butter,
    chopped
1 egg
2 tablespoons sesame seeds

Spinach and Ricotta Filling
50 g (1³/₄ oz) butter
1 cup (125 g/4 oz) finely
    chopped spring onions
2 cloves garlic, crushed
500 g (1 lb) English spinach,
    trimmed, washed and roughly
    shredded
2 tablespoons chopped mint
³/₄ cup (185 g/6 oz) ricotta
    cheese
¹/₂ cup (50 g/1³/₄ oz) freshly
    grated Parmesan
3 eggs, beaten
1–2 tablespoons milk

1 Place the flour and butter in a food processor and process for 15 seconds, or until the mixture resembles fine breadcrumbs. Add the egg, sesame seeds and 2–3 tablespoons of water. Process in short bursts until the mixture just comes together, adding a little extra water if necessary. Turn out onto a lightly floured surface and quickly gather into a ball. Cover the pastry with plastic wrap and refrigerate for at least 15 minutes. Place a baking tray in the oven and preheat the oven to moderate 180°C (350°F/Gas 4).

2 To make the filling, melt the butter in a large pan, add the spring onions and garlic and cook until soft. Add the spinach a little at a time, then stir in the mint. Remove from the heat and allow to cool slightly before stirring in the ricotta, Parmesan and the beaten eggs. Season to taste with salt and some freshly ground black pepper and mix well.

3 Grease a shallow 23 cm (9 inch) loose-based flan tin. Take two-thirds of the pastry and, on a sheet of baking paper, roll it out thinly to line the tin, pressing it well into the sides. Fill the pastry shell with the spinach and ricotta filling.

4 Roll out the remaining pastry and cut into 1.5 cm (⁵/₈ inch) strips. Interweave the pastry strips in a lattice pattern over the top of the tart. Dampen the edge of the pastry base and gently press the strips down. Trim the edges of the pastry by pressing down with your thumb or by rolling a rolling pin across the top of the tin. Then brush with milk. Place on the heated baking tray and bake for about 40 minutes, or until the pastry is golden.

NUTRITION PER SERVE
Protein 20 g; Fat 35 g; Carbohydrate 35 g; Dietary Fibre 5 g; Cholesterol 215 mg; 2220 kJ (530 cal)

COOK'S FILE

Note: Depending on how thick you like to roll your pastry, there may be about 100 g (3¹/₂ oz) of pastry trimmings left over. It is easier to have this little bit extra when making the lattice strips as they will be long enough to cover the top of the pie. The extra pastry can be covered and frozen for future use as decorations, or made into small tart shells.

Wash spinach very thoroughly as it can be gritty, then trim and roughly shred.

Allow the filling mixture to cool a little before adding the cheeses and egg.

Lift pastry into a tin by draping it over the rolling pin and removing the paper.

Roll out the remaining pastry and cut into thin strips for the lattice.

Interweave the lattice strips over the top of the filling.

Dampen the edge of the pastry shell, press down the lattice and trim.

BEETROOT AND FETA TART

Preparation time: 40 minutes
 + 15 minutes refrigeration
Total cooking time: 55 minutes
Serves 6

3/4 cup (90 g/3 oz) plain
 wholemeal flour
3/4 cup (90 g/3 oz) plain flour
125 g (4 oz) cold butter,
 chopped
1 egg yolk

Filling
300 g (10 oz) ricotta cheese
300 g (10 oz) Bulgarian feta
 cheese, crumbled
3 eggs, lightly beaten
300 g (10 oz) baby beetroots,
 with short stalks attached
1 tablespoon walnut or olive oil
1 tablespoon red wine vinegar
1/4 cup (30 g/1 oz) roughly
 chopped pecans
2 tablespoons coriander leaves

1 Place the flours, butter and a pinch of salt in a food processor and mix for 15 seconds, or until crumbly. Add the egg yolk and 1–2 tablespoons of cold water. Process in short bursts until the mixture just comes together, adding a little more water if needed. Turn out onto a floured surface and quickly gather together into a ball. Cover with plastic wrap and chill for 15 minutes. Preheat the oven to moderate 180°C (350°F/Gas 4).
2 Mix together the ricotta and feta with a fork. Add the eggs and mix well. Grease a 23 cm (9 inch) loose-based flan tin. Roll out the pastry on a floured surface to line the tin, pressing

it well into the sides. Using a sharp knife, trim off any excess pastry. Cover with baking paper, fill with baking beads or rice and bake for 10 minutes. Remove the paper and beads and bake for 10 minutes. Spoon the filling into the base and cook for 30 minutes, or until the filling is firm and puffed (it will flatten after being removed from the oven).

3 Boil or steam the trimmed beetroots until tender, peel, then cut in half. Drizzle with the combined oil and vinegar, and season to taste. Arrange the warm beetroot pieces over the tart and scatter with pecans and coriander.

NUTRITION PER SERVE
Protein 25 g; Fat 45 g; Carbohydrate 25 g; Dietary Fibre 4 g; Cholesterol 230 mg; 2455 kJ (585 cal)

Baby beetroots should be well scrubbed and trimmed, leaving just a short stem.

Process the flours and butter until the mixture resembles fine breadcrumbs.

Blind bake the pastry shell, then add the ricotta and feta filling.

COUNTRY TOMATO AND THYME TART

Preparation time: 35 minutes
+ 15 minutes refrigeration
Total cooking time: 30 minutes
Serves 6

Cream Cheese Pastry
2 cups (250 g/8 oz) plain flour
125 g (4 oz) cold butter,
  chopped
125 g (4 oz) cream cheese,
  chopped
1 tablespoon thyme leaves

1/2 cup (40 g/1 1/4 oz) fresh
  breadcrumbs
1/3 cup (35 g/1 1/4 oz) freshly
  grated Parmesan
2 tablespoons lemon thyme
  leaves
6 Roma tomatoes, sliced
3 spring onions, sliced

1 egg yolk, beaten with
  1 teaspoon of water, to glaze

1 Place the flour, butter, cream cheese and thyme in a food processor and process well. Add 2 tablespoons of water and process in short bursts until the mixture just comes together, adding more water if needed. Turn out onto a floured surface and quickly gather together into a ball. Press the pastry dough into a large triangle. Cover with plastic wrap and chill for 15 minutes. Place on a greased baking tray and prick all over with a fork.
2 Preheat the oven to hot 210°C (415°F/Gas 6–7). Place the breadcrumbs, most of the Parmesan and 1 tablespoon of lemon thyme on the pastry, leaving an 8 cm (3 inch)

border. Overlap the tomatoes and some of the spring onions on top, keeping the border. Add freshly ground black pepper, the remaining spring onions, Parmesan and lemon thyme. Fold the pastry border over, pleating as you go, and press to seal. Brush the pastry with the beaten egg

yolk and water. Bake for 10 minutes, reduce the oven to moderate 180°C (350°F/Gas 4) and cook for 15–20 minutes, or until golden.

NUTRITION PER SERVE
Protein 10 g; Fat 30 g; Carbohydrate 40 g; Dietary Fibre 3 g; Cholesterol 110 mg; 1840 kJ (440 cal)

Cut the Roma tomatoes into slices about 1 cm (1/2 inch) wide.

Press the pastry dough into a rough triangle shape before chilling.

Turn the pastry border up and over to make a traditional freeform tart.

CHEESE AND CHIVE SOUFFLE TART

Preparation time: 40 minutes
Total cooking time: 55 minutes
Serves 6–8

80 g (2¾ oz) butter
⅓ cup (40 g/1¼ oz) sifted flour
1 cup (250 ml/8 fl oz) cream
⅔ cup (170 ml/5½ fl oz) sour cream
4 eggs, separated
1 cup (130 g/4½ oz) grated Gruyère cheese
3 tablespoons chopped chives
¼ teaspoon ground nutmeg

pinch of cayenne pepper
12 sheets filo pastry

1 Preheat the oven to moderately hot 190°C (375°F/Gas 5). Grease a deep loose-based fluted flan tin measuring 20 cm (8 inches) across the base. Melt half the butter in a pan. Add the flour and cook, stirring, for 1 minute. Remove from the heat and gradually whisk in the cream and sour cream.
2 Return to the heat and whisk constantly until the mixture boils and thickens. Remove from the heat and whisk in the egg yolks. Then cover with plastic wrap and set aside to allow to cool slightly. Whisk in the cheese, chives, nutmeg and cayenne.

3 Melt the remaining butter and brush some over each sheet of pastry. Fold each one in half and use to line the tin, allowing the edges to overhang.
4 Beat the egg whites until stiff peaks form, then stir a spoonful into the cheese mixture. Gently fold in the rest. Spoon the mixture into the pastry shell and then fold the pastry over the top. Brush the top with the remaining melted butter and bake for 40–45 minutes, or until puffed and golden. Serve immediately.

NUTRITION PER SERVE (8)
Protein 10 g; Fat 40 g; Carbohydrate 15 g; Dietary Fibre 1 g; Cholesterol 200 mg; 1895 kJ (450 cal)

Fold each buttered sheet of filo in half, and use to line the flan tin.

Fold a spoonful of the beaten egg white into the cheese mixture.

Carefully fold the filo pastry over the top of the filling.

CHICKEN AND MUSHROOM PITHIVER

Preparation time: 45 minutes
+ 30 minutes refrigeration
Total cooking time: 40 minutes
Serves 4

50 g (1³/4 oz) butter
2 rashers bacon, sliced
4 spring onions, chopped
100 g (3¹/2 oz) button
    mushrooms, sliced
1 tablespoon plain flour
³/4 cup (185 ml/6 fl oz) milk
1 tablespoon cream
1 cup (180 g/6 oz) chopped
    cooked chicken breast
¹/3 cup (20 g/³/4 oz) chopped
    parsley

2 sheets ready-rolled puff pastry
1 egg yolk, lightly beaten,
    to glaze

1 Melt the butter in a pan and cook the bacon and spring onions, stirring, for 2–3 minutes. Add the mushrooms and cook, stirring, for 3 minutes. Stir in the flour and cook for 1 minute. Add the milk all at once and stir for 2–3 minutes, or until thickened. Simmer for 1 minute then remove from the heat. Stir in the cream, chicken and parsley. Set aside to cool.
2 Cut two 23 cm (9 inch) circles from the pastry sheets, using a dinner plate or cake tin as a guide. Place 1 circle on a greased baking tray. Pile the chicken filling into the centre of the pastry, mounding slightly in the centre and leaving a 2 cm (³/4 inch) border. Combine the egg yolk with 1 teaspoon of water, and brush the pastry border.

3 Using a small pointed knife, and starting from the centre of the second circle, mark curved lines at regular intervals. Take care not to cut through the pastry. Place this sheet over the other and stretch a little to fit evenly. Press the edges together to seal. Using the back of a knife, push up the outside edge at 1 cm (¹/2 inch) intervals. Cover and refrigerate for at least 30 minutes. Preheat the oven to moderately hot 190°C (375°F/Gas 5). Brush the tart with the egg mixture and make a small hole in the centre for steam to escape. Bake for 25 minutes, or until golden.

NUTRITION PER SERVE
Protein 25 g; Fat 40 g; Carbohydrate 35 g; Dietary Fibre 2 g; Cholesterol 160 mg; 2395 kJ (570 cal)

Stir the cream, chicken and chopped parsley into the filling mixture.

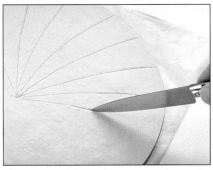
Draw curved lines from the centre to the edge of the pastry.

Use the back of a knife to push up the edge of the pastry.

PISSALADIERE

Preparation time: 50 minutes
 + 30 minutes refrigeration
Total cooking time: 2 hours 40 minutes
Serves 4

Pastry
2 cups (250 g/8 oz) plain flour
185 g (6 oz) cold butter, chopped
1 egg yolk
1 teaspoon lemon juice

Onion Topping
1/3 cup (80 ml/2³/4 fl oz) olive oil
6 large onions, thinly sliced
2–3 cloves garlic, crushed
425 g (14 oz) can chopped
    tomatoes
2 teaspoons caster sugar
1/4 cup (15 g/1/2 oz) chopped
    parsley
1 tablespoon chopped thyme
1 tablespoon chopped oregano
1 tablespoon tomato paste
2 x 45 g (1¹/2 oz) cans anchovies,
    drained
40 small black olives
2 teaspoons olive oil, extra

1 To make the pastry, place the flour and butter in a food processor and process for 15 seconds, or until the mixture resembles fine breadcrumbs. Add the combined egg yolk, lemon juice and 3 tablespoons of cold water. Process in short bursts until the mixture just comes together, adding a little more water if necessary. Turn the mixture out onto a floured surface and gather together into a ball. Cover the dough with plastic wrap and refrigerate for at least 15 minutes.
2 To make the onion topping, heat the oil in a large pan and add the onion and garlic. Cover and cook over low heat, stirring frequently, for 40 minutes, but do not overbrown. Uncover and cook, stirring frequently, for a further 30–40 minutes, or until the onion is very soft.
3 Put the tomatoes and sugar in a pan and cook, stirring, over medium heat for 30–40 minutes, or until thick and pulpy and reduced to about 3/4 cup (185 ml/6 fl oz). Take care not to burn. Stir in the parsley, thyme, oregano, tomato paste and pepper to taste. Set aside to cool, then stir into the onion mixture.
4 Preheat the oven to moderately hot 190°C (375°F/Gas 5). Grease 2 baking trays. Divide the pastry in half and roll each into an oval about 35 x 20 cm (14 x 8 inches). Place on the trays and turn over a thin border from the outside edge. Prick well with a fork, cover and refrigerate for at least 15 minutes. Bake for 15–20 minutes, or until lightly browned and crisp.
5 Increase the oven temperature to moderately hot 200°C (400°F/Gas 6). Spread the onion and tomato mixture evenly over the pastry ovals. Cut the anchovies in half lengthways and arrange over the top to make a diamond pattern. Place an olive in the centre of each anchovy diamond. Lightly drizzle with the extra oil. Bake for 20 minutes. Serve hot or at room temperature.

NUTRITION PER SERVE
Protein 20 g; Fat 70 g; Carbohydrate 60 g; Dietary Fibre 8 g; Cholesterol 180 mg; 3940 kJ (940 cal)

COOK'S FILE

Note: If you prefer anchovies less salty, soak them in cold milk for 5 minutes.

Slice the onions thinly across their equators so they hold together in rings.

Cook the onion rings and garlic, stirring frequently, until very soft but not brown.

Stir the herbs and tomato paste into the thick tomato and sugar mixture.

Put the pastry ovals on the greased trays and turn over a thin border.

Slice the anchovies in half lengthways to make thin strips for the lattice.

Arrange the anchovy strips over the top of the pissaladière.

ROASTED VEGETABLE AND FETA TARTS

Preparation time: 1 hour
Total cooking time: 1 hour
Serves 6

1 small red capsicum, cubed
1 small yellow capsicum, cubed
300 g (10 oz) eggplant, cubed
2 zucchini, sliced
125 g (4 oz) cherry tomatoes
3 cloves garlic, crushed
2 tablespoons olive oil
1 teaspoon cumin seeds
3–4 sheets ready-rolled
    shortcrust pastry
300 g (10 oz) feta cheese
300 g (10 oz) ricotta cheese
2 teaspoons balsamic vinegar
1 tablespoon chopped parsley

1 Preheat the oven to moderately hot 200°C (400°F/Gas 6). Place the capsicum, eggplant, zucchini and tomatoes in a baking dish lined with baking paper. Mix together the garlic, olive oil, cumin seeds and a pinch of salt. Drizzle over the vegetables. Roast for about 30 minutes, or until tender.
2 Line twelve 8 cm (3 inch) fluted loose-based flan tins with the pastry, pressing it well into the sides, and trim off any excess. Prick the bases with a fork and bake for 10 minutes, or until cooked and golden.
3 Mash together the feta and ricotta cheeses with a fork until smooth. Spoon into the tart shells and smooth with the back of a spoon dipped in hot water. Bake for 15–20 minutes, or until golden and warmed through.
4 Drizzle the balsamic vinegar over the roasted vegetables and mix well. Then spoon into each cooked tart and sprinkle with parsley.

NUTRITION PER SERVE
Protein 25 g; Fat 50 g; Carbohydrate 50 g; Dietary Fibre 5 g; Cholesterol 90 mg; 3070 kJ (730 cal)

COOK'S FILE

Hint: If you roll out all the trimmings from the pastry to line some of the tins you should only need to use 3 sheets of ready-rolled shortcrust pastry overall, otherwise use 4 sheets and keep the trimmings for another recipe.

Cut the vegetables into small cubes before roasting.

Drizzle the flavoured oil over the chopped vegetables and roast until tender.

Prick the pastry bases all over with a fork and bake until golden.

Smooth the cheese filling with the back of a spoon dipped in hot water.

CARAMELISED ONION, MUSHROOM AND GOAT'S CHEESE TART

Preparation time: 40 minutes
 + 35 minutes refrigeration
Total cooking time: 1 hour 35 minutes
Serves 6

2 cups (250 g/8 oz) plain flour
125 g (4 oz) cold butter,
    chopped
1/2 cup (125 g/4 oz) ricotta
    cheese

Filling
50 g (1³/4 oz) butter
3 onions, thinly sliced
200 g (6¹/2 oz) button
    mushrooms, sliced
100 g (3¹/2 oz) goat's cheese,
    crumbled
1/2 cup (125 g/4 oz) ricotta
    cheese
1 tablespoon thyme leaves

1 Put the flour, butter and ricotta in a food processor and process for 15 seconds, or until well mixed. Add 2 tablespoons of water. Process in short bursts until the mixture just comes together, adding a little more water if necessary. Turn out onto a floured surface and gather together into a ball. Cover with plastic wrap and refrigerate for at least 15 minutes.
2 To make the filling, heat the butter in a large pan, add the onion and cook over low heat, stirring frequently, for 40–45 minutes, or until golden brown. Add the mushrooms and stir over the heat for a further 10 minutes. Drain and leave to cool. Stir through the crumbled goat's cheese, ricotta and thyme leaves.

3 Roll out the pastry on a sheet of baking paper to a 32 cm (13 inch) circle and place on a large, greased pizza tray. Turn over the outside edge to make a small rim, pressing to seal. Prick the base all over with a fork, cover and refrigerate for 20 minutes.
4 Preheat the oven to moderately hot

200°C (400°F/Gas 6). Bake the base for 15 minutes, reduce the oven to moderate 180°C (350°F/Gas 4). Add the filling and bake for 25 minutes.

NUTRITION PER SERVE
Protein 15 g; Fat 35 g; Carbohydrate 35 g; Dietary Fibre 3 g; Cholesterol 105 mg; 2050 kJ (490 cal)

Cook the onion slowly, until caramelised, then add the mushroom.

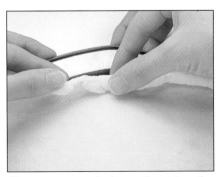

Turn over a small rim on the outer edge of the pastry base.

Pricking the pastry base all over prevents it rising unevenly during cooking.

Finger Foods

HUMMUS AND TOMATO SALSA BOATS

Roll 2 sheets of ready-rolled shortcrust pastry into 27 cm (10¾ inch) squares. Cut each sheet into 8 rectangles and fit into greased 10 cm (4 inch) long pastry boat tins. Prick all over with a fork, cover and chill for 10–15 minutes. Bake at moderately hot 190°C (375°F/Gas 5) for 8–10 minutes, then cool. Seed and dice 2 firm Roma tomatoes and mix with ½ diced avocado, 1 crushed garlic clove and 1 tablespoon each of chopped chives and coriander. Drizzle with a teaspoon each of olive oil and balsamic vinegar. Spread hummus over the base of the boats, pile the salsa on top and decorate with a coriander leaf. Makes 16.

NUTRITION PER PASTRY
Protein 2 g; Fat 8 g; Carbohydrate 8 g; Dietary Fibre 1 g; Cholesterol 5 mg; 460 kJ (110 cal)

PROSCIUTTO AND BASIL PINWHEELS

Mix 2 tablespoons of soft cream cheese with 2 tablespoons coarsely grated Parmesan, 1 tablespoon pesto and 1 tablespoon each of chopped chives and basil. Spread over 2 sheets of ready-rolled puff pastry, leaving a 2 cm (¾ inch) border. Place 3 slices of prosciutto over each sheet of pastry, then roll up and seal the edge with beaten egg. Cut each roll into 2 cm (¾ inch) slices. Place on a greased baking tray and flatten to 1 cm (½ inch). Brush with beaten egg and bake at moderately hot 190°C (375°F/Gas 5) for 15 minutes, or until puffed and golden. Makes about 30.

NUTRITION PER PASTRY
Protein 1 g; Fat 1 g; Carbohydrate 0 g; Dietary Fibre 0 g; Cholesterol 10 mg; 80 kJ (20 cal)

SMOKED TROUT WITH HORSERADISH CREAM TARTLETS

Roll 2 sheets of ready-rolled shortcrust pastry into 27 cm (10¾ inch) squares. Using a 5.5 cm (2¼ inch) plain or fluted cutter, cut 18 rounds from each sheet. Fit the pastry rounds into mini muffin tins. Prick well with a fork, refrigerate for 15 minutes, and bake in a moderately hot 190°C (375°F/ Gas 5) oven for 8–10 minutes. Skin and bone a 230 g (7½ oz) smoked trout. Combine ¾ cup (185 ml/6 fl oz) sour cream with 1 tablespoon of horseradish cream and 1 teaspoon lemon juice and season to taste. Rinse and dry 3 tablespoons baby capers. Put a teaspoon of the filling into each pastry and top with 2–3 small pieces of trout, a few capers and a sprig of fennel, or chopped chives. Makes 36.

NUTRITION PER PASTRY
Protein 2 g; Fat 5 g; Carbohydrate 5 g; Dietary Fibre 0 g; Cholesterol 15 mg; 305 kJ (70 cal)

RATATOUILLE TRIANGLES

Fry 1 finely chopped spring onion and 1–2 crushed garlic cloves in a little oil for 2 minutes. Add 1 diced eggplant, 1 diced red capsicum, 2 diced zucchini, 6 diced button mushrooms and cook, stirring, for 10 minutes, or until softened. Remove from the heat and add 1 peeled, seeded and chopped tomato, 1 tablespoon chopped capers and 2 tablespoons chopped parsley. Cool and add 50 g (1 3/4 oz) grated Parmesan. Take 2 sheets of ready-rolled puff pastry, cut each sheet into 3 equal strips and each strip into 3 triangles. Roll up a thin border on each side of the triangle and twist the corners to seal. Place on a greased baking tray and prick all over using a fork. Cover and chill for 10–15 minutes. Bake at moderately hot 190°C (375°F/Gas 5) for 15 minutes, or until crisp. Place a tablespoon of filling into each pastry and reheat for 5–10 minutes. Makes 18.

NUTRITION PER PASTRY
Protein 3 g; Fat 7 g; Carbohydrate 8 g; Dietary Fibre 1 g; Cholesterol 7 mg; 450 kJ (105 cal)

SMOKED SALMON WITH HERBED CREME FRAICHE TARTLETS

Roll 2 sheets of ready-rolled shortcrust pastry into 27 cm (10 3/4 inch) squares. Using a 5.5 cm (2 1/4 inch) cutter, cut 18 rounds from each sheet. Fit the pastry rounds into mini muffin tins. Prick well, chill for 10–15 minutes and bake at moderately hot 190°C (375°F/Gas 5) for 8–10 minutes. Cut 200 g (6 1/2 oz) of smoked salmon into strips. Combine 200 ml (6 1/2 fl oz) of crème fraîche with 1 1/2 tablespoons each of chopped chives and dill, 1/2 teaspoon lemon rind, 1 teaspoon lemon juice and season to taste. Cut a small red onion into thin rings. To assemble the tartlets, place a teaspoon of filling into each pastry case and pile strips of salmon on top. Finish with an onion ring, a sprig of dill and some salmon eggs. Serve immediately. Makes 36.

NUTRITION PER PASTRY
Protein 2 g; Fat 5 g; Carbohydrate 4 g; Dietary Fibre 0 g; Cholesterol 15 mg; 295 kJ (70 cal)

HERBED GOAT'S CHEESE PASTRIES

Mix 150 g (5 oz) crumbled goat's cheese with 1 finely chopped spring onion, 1 tablespoon olive oil, 1 tablespoon each of chopped parsley and chives, 1 crushed garlic clove and 1/4 teaspoon dried oregano leaves. Take 4 sheets of ready-rolled puff pastry and, using a 5.5 cm (2 1/4 inch) cutter, cut 16 rounds from each sheet. Place half on greased baking trays and brush the edges with beaten egg. Place a teaspoon of filling in the centre of each and top with the other rounds. Seal each pastry by pressing with a fork and then prick the top. Cover and chill for 10–15 minutes. Brush with beaten egg and bake at moderately hot 190°C (375°F/Gas 5) for 12–15 minutes, until puffed. Makes 32.

NUTRITION PER PASTRY
Protein 2 g; Fat 7 g; Carbohydrate 8 g; Dietary Fibre 0 g; Cholesterol 15 mg; 410 kJ (95 cal)

From left: Hummus and Tomato Salsa Boats; Smoked Trout with Horseradish Cream; Prosciutto and Basil Pinwheels; Ratatouille Triangles; Smoked Salmon with Herbed Crème Fraîche; Herbed Goat's Cheese Pastries

SALAMI, EGGPLANT AND ARTICHOKE TART

Preparation time: 20 minutes
+ 30 minutes refrigeration
Total cooking time: 50 minutes
Serves 4–6

1 cup (125 g/4 oz) plain flour
60 g (2 oz) cold butter, chopped
1 egg yolk

Filling
2 tablespoons oil
250 g (8 oz) eggplant, cubed
125 g (4 oz) piece salami, cubed
1/2 cup (110 g/3 1/2 oz) quartered
   marinated artichokes

1 tablespoon chopped chives
1 tablespoon chopped parsley
1 egg, lightly beaten
1/4 cup (60 ml/2 fl oz) cream

1 Put the flour and butter in a food processor and process for 15 seconds, or until crumbly. Add the egg yolk and 1–2 tablespoons of water and process in short bursts until the mixture just comes together, adding a little more water if necessary. Turn the mixture out onto a floured surface and gather together into a ball. Cover with plastic wrap and refrigerate for at least 20 minutes. Preheat the oven to moderately hot 200°C (400°F/ Gas 6). Grease a shallow 20 cm (8 inch) loose-based flan tin.

2 Roll out the pastry on a sheet of baking paper to line the tin and trim off any excess. Refrigerate for 10 minutes. Prick the pastry with a fork and bake for 10 minutes, or until lightly browned. Cool.

3 To make the filling, heat the oil and toss the eggplant over high heat until it begins to brown and soften; drain on paper towels. Combine the salami, eggplant, artichokes and herbs and press firmly into the pastry case. Pour over the combined egg and cream mixture and bake for 35 minutes, or until browned and set.

NUTRITION PER SERVE (6)
Protein 8 g; Fat 25 g; Carbohydrate 15 g; Dietary Fibre 2 g; Cholesterol 75 mg; 1300 kJ (310 cal)

Cut the salami and eggplant into cubes. You can use plain or flat-leaf parsley.

Toss the eggplant over high heat until it begins to brown and soften.

Press the filling firmly into the base and pour over the egg and cream.

FRESH HERB TART

Total preparation time: 40 minutes
+ 30 minutes refrigeration
Total cooking time: 1 hour 15 minutes
Serves 4–6

1¼ cups (150 g/5 oz) plain flour
100 g (3½ oz) cold butter,
    cubed

250 g (8 oz) light sour cream
½ cup (125 ml/4 fl oz) thick
    cream
2 eggs, lightly beaten
1 tablespoon chopped thyme
2 tablespoons chopped parsley
1 tablespoon chopped oregano

1 Put the flour and butter in a food processor and process for 15 seconds, or until the mixture resembles fine breadcrumbs. Add 1–2 tablespoons of cold water and process in short bursts until the mixture just comes together, adding a little more water if needed. Turn out onto a floured surface and gather together into a ball. Cover with plastic wrap and refrigerate for at least 20 minutes. Roll out on a sheet of baking paper to line a 34 x 10 cm (14 x 4 inch) loose-based flan tin. Trim off any excess pastry with a sharp knife or by rolling a rolling pin across the top of the tin. Chill for 10 minutes. Preheat the oven to moderately hot 200°C (400°F/Gas 6).

2 Cover the pastry shell with baking paper and fill evenly with baking beads. Place on a baking tray and bake for 20 minutes. Remove the paper and beads and reduce the oven to moderate 180°C (350°F/Gas 4). Cook for a further 15–20 minutes, or until dry and lightly coloured. Cool.

3 Whisk together the sour cream, thick cream and eggs until smooth. Then stir through the herbs. Season with salt and freshly cracked pepper.

4 Place the pastry shell on a baking tray and pour in the filling. Bake for 25–30 minutes, or until set. Allow to stand for 15 minutes before serving.

NUTRITION PER SERVE (6)
Protein 6 g; Fat 25 g; Carbohydrate 20 g; Dietary Fibre 1 g; Cholesterol 130 mg; 1340 kJ (320 cal)

If you don't have baking beads for blind baking, use dry rice or beans.

Put the sour cream, thick cream and eggs in a bowl and whisk together.

Put the pastry shell on a baking tray before cooking to catch any drips.

MUSHROOM AND RICOTTA FILO TART

Preparation time: 35 minutes
Total cooking time: 40 minutes
Serves 6

60 g (2 oz) butter
270 g (9 oz) field mushrooms, sliced
2 cloves garlic, crushed
1 tablespoon Marsala
1 teaspoon thyme leaves
1/2 teaspoon chopped rosemary leaves
pinch of freshly grated nutmeg
5 sheets filo pastry
75 g (2 1/2 oz) butter, melted
200 g (6 1/2 oz) ricotta cheese
2 eggs, lightly beaten
1/2 cup (125 ml/4 fl oz) sour cream
1 tablespoon chopped parsley

1 Preheat the oven to moderate 180°C (350°F/Gas 4). Melt the butter in a frying pan and add the mushrooms. Cook over high heat for a few minutes, until they begin to soften. Add the garlic and cook for another minute. Stir in the Marsala, thyme, rosemary and nutmeg. Remove the mushrooms from the pan and drain off any liquid.

2 Work with 1 sheet of filo pastry at a time, keeping the rest covered with a damp tea towel to stop them drying out. Brush the sheets with melted butter and fold in half. Place on top of each other to line a shallow 23 cm (9 inch) loose-based flan tin, allowing the edges to overhang.

3 Beat the ricotta, eggs and cream together and season to taste. Spoon half the mixture into the tin, then add the mushrooms. Top with the rest of the ricotta mixture. Bake for 35 minutes, or until firm. Sprinkle with the chopped parsley.

NUTRITION PER SERVE
Protein 9 g; Fat 35 g; Carbohydrate 9 g; Dietary Fibre 2 g; Cholesterol 160 mg; 1515 kJ (360 cal)

Remove the mushrooms from the pan, draining off as much liquid as possible.

Layer half the ricotta filling into the pastry, then the mushroom mixture.

Brush the filo with melted butter, fold in half and layer into the tin.

SPICY CHICKEN TARTS

Preparation time: 50 minutes
Total cooking time: 45 minutes
Makes 8

2 large onions, finely chopped
400 g (13 oz) eggplant, cubed
2 cloves garlic, crushed
2 x 410 g (13 oz) cans chopped
   tomatoes
1 tablespoon tomato paste
3 teaspoons soft brown sugar
1 tablespoon red wine vinegar
3 tablespoons chopped parsley
4 sheets ready-rolled shortcrust
   pastry

2 teaspoons ground cumin seeds
2 teaspoons ground coriander
1 teaspoon paprika
400 g (13 oz) chicken breast
   fillets
sour cream and coriander leaves

1 Fry the onion in a little oil until golden. Add the eggplant and garlic and cook for a few minutes. Stir in the tomatoes, tomato paste, sugar and vinegar. Bring to the boil, reduce the heat, cover and simmer for 20 minutes. Uncover and simmer for 10 minutes, or until thick. Add the parsley and season. Preheat the oven to moderately hot 190°C (375°F/Gas 5).
2 Grease 8 small pie tins measuring

7.5 cm (3 inches) across the base, line with the pastry and decorate the edges with a spoon. Prick the bases using a fork. Bake for 15 minutes, or until golden.
3 Mix the cumin, coriander and paprika on greaseproof paper. Coat the chicken pieces in the spices. Heat some oil in a frying pan and cook the chicken until brown and cooked through. Cut diagonally. Fill the pie shells with the eggplant mixture and add the chicken, sour cream and coriander leaves.

NUTRITION PER SERVE
Protein 20 g; Fat 35 g; Carbohydrate 45 g
Dietary Fibre 5 g; Cholesterol 65 mg;
2315 kJ (550 cal)

Simmer the tomato mixture uncovered to reduce the liquid, then add the parsley.

It is quick and simple to decorate the edge of the pastry case with a spoon.

Detach the tenderloin from the breast as it will cook much more quickly.

SPICY PUMPKIN AND CASHEW TARTS

Preparation time: 1 hour
 + 20 minutes refrigeration
Total cooking time: 1 hour
Serves 4

2 cups (250 g/8 oz) plain flour
100 g (3¹/2 oz) cold butter,
    chopped
1¹/2 tablespoons coriander
    seeds, lightly crushed
1 egg

Cashew Nut Topping
¹/4 cup (40 g/1¹/4 oz) roasted
    cashews, chopped
¹/4 teaspoon paprika
1 teaspoon cumin seeds
1 teaspoon sesame seeds

Spicy Pumpkin Filling
600 g (1 lb 4 oz) butternut
    pumpkin
1 tablespoon oil
1 onion, thinly sliced
1 clove garlic, crushed
¹/4 teaspoon ground cumin
¹/4 teaspoon ground coriander
¹/2 teaspoon garam masala
¹/4 teaspoon chilli flakes
1 tablespoon honey
1 tablespoon soy sauce
200 g (6¹/2 oz) ricotta cheese

1 Place the flour, butter, coriander seeds and a pinch of salt in a food processor and process for 15 seconds, or until the mixture resembles fine breadcrumbs. Add the egg and 2 teaspoons of water. Process in short bursts until the mixture just comes together, adding a little more water if necessary. Turn out onto a floured surface and gather together into a ball. Cover with plastic wrap and refrigerate for at least 20 minutes.

2 Preheat the oven to moderately hot 200°C (400°F/Gas 6). Grease 4 shallow 11 cm (4¹/2 inch) loose-based flan tins. Divide the pastry into quarters and roll out on a sheet of baking paper to line the tins, pressing well into the base and sides. Trim off the excess pastry with a sharp knife or by rolling a rolling pin over the top of the tin. Prick all over the bases with a fork and bake for 18–20 minutes, or until browned. Set aside to cool. Reduce the oven temperature to moderate 180°C (350°F/Gas 4).

3 To make the cashew nut topping, combine the cashews and paprika in a small bowl. Place the cumin and sesame seeds in a dry frying pan and stir over low heat until lightly toasted, add to the cashew mixture and set aside to cool.

4 To make the spicy pumpkin filling, cut the pumpkin into 2.5 cm (1 inch) pieces. Heat the oil in a pan, add the pumpkin, onion, garlic and spices and cook, stirring, over medium heat, until the onion is soft and translucent. Add the honey and 2 tablespoons of water. Bring to the boil, then reduce the heat and simmer, covered, for 10–15 minutes, or until the pumpkin is tender. Stir in the soy sauce.

5 Place a quarter of the ricotta cheese into the base of each pastry shell. Spoon the spicy pumpkin filling and its liquid over the cheese and then sprinkle with the cashew nut topping. Place the tarts in the oven to reheat for 10 minutes. Serve warm.

NUTRITION PER SERVE
Protein 20 g; Fat 40 g; Carbohydrate 70 g; Dietary Fibre 6 g; Cholesterol 135 mg; 2955 kJ (705 cal)

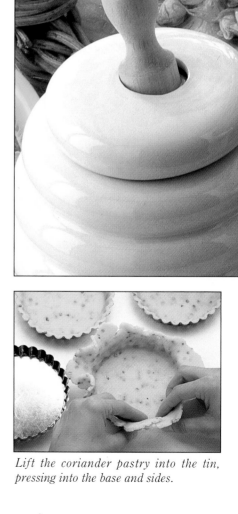

Lightly crush the coriander seeds in a mortar and pestle.

Chop the roasted cashew nuts and then mix with the paprika in a bowl.

Lift the coriander pastry into the tin, pressing into the base and sides.

Trim off the excess pastry and then prick all over the base of the pastry case.

Fry the cumin and sesame seeds in a dry frying pan.

Add the honey and water and then bring the pumpkin filling to the boil.

GOAT'S CHEESE AND SWEET POTATO TART

Preparation time: 30 minutes
+ 30 minutes refrigeration
Total cooking time: 40 minutes
Serves 2–3

2 teaspoons fine semolina
1 cup (125 g/4 oz) self-raising
   flour
60 g (2 oz) cold butter, chopped
1 egg yolk

Leek and Sweet Potato Filling
2 tablespoons olive oil
1 small leek, chopped
50 g (1¾ oz) soft goat's cheese,
   crumbled
1 egg, lightly beaten
2 tablespoons cream
150 g (5 oz) orange sweet
   potato, thinly sliced
½ teaspoon cumin seeds

1 Lightly grease a 25 cm (10 inch) pizza tray or baking tray and sprinkle with the semolina.
2 Put the flour and butter in a food processor and process for 15 seconds, or until the mixture resembles fine breadcrumbs. Add the egg yolk and 2 tablespoons of water. Process in short bursts until the mixture just comes together, adding a little extra water if necessary. Turn out onto a floured surface and gather together into a ball. Cover with plastic wrap and chill for 20 minutes.
3 Roll out the dough to a 20 cm (8 inch) circle. Lift onto the tray and roll over the outside edge to make a small rim; pinch this decoratively with your fingers. Prick the base with a fork and refrigerate for 10 minutes.

Preheat the oven to moderately hot 200°C (400°F/Gas 6). Bake for 12 minutes, or until just brown.
4 Heat half the oil in a pan, add the leek and cook until soft, then allow to cool. Spread the leek over the base of the pastry case, top with the crumbled cheese and season to taste. Pour over the combined egg and cream and lay

the sweet potato on top. Brush with the remaining oil and add the cumin seeds. Bake for 20–25 minutes, or until the filling is set. Leave for 5 minutes before cutting.

NUTRITION PER SERVE (3)
Protein 15 g; Fat 45 g; Carbohydrate 40 g; Dietary Fibre 3 g; Cholesterol 200 mg; 2475 kJ (590 cal)

Peel the orange sweet potato and slice very thinly.

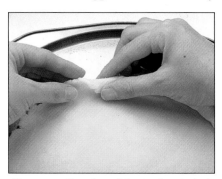

Turn over the edge of the pastry circle to make a small rim.

Pinch the rim between your fingers to make a decorative edging.

ROASTED TOMATO AND GARLIC TART

Preparation time: 40 minutes
Total cooking time: 1 hour 10 minutes
Serves 4

4 Roma tomatoes, halved
1 tablespoon olive oil
1 teaspoon balsamic vinegar
1 teaspoon salt
5–10 unpeeled cloves garlic
2 sheets ready-rolled puff
   pastry

1 egg, lightly beaten
10 bocconcini, halved
small basil leaves, to garnish

1 Preheat the oven to moderately hot 200°C (400°F/Gas 6). Put the tomatoes, cut-side-up, on a baking tray and drizzle with the olive oil, balsamic vinegar and salt. Bake for 20 minutes. Add the garlic and bake for a further 15 minutes. Cool and squeeze or peel the garlic from its skin.
2 Grease a 34 x 10 cm (13½ x 4 inch) loose-based fluted flan tin. Lay a sheet of pastry over each end of the tin, so

that they overlap the edges and each other. Seal the sheets together with egg and trim the edges. Cover with baking paper and baking beads. Bake for 15 minutes. Remove the paper and beads and bake for 10 minutes.
3 Place the roasted tomatoes along the centre of the tart and fill the gaps with the garlic and halved bocconcini. Bake for a further 10 minutes and serve with basil leaves.

NUTRITION PER SERVE
Protein 25 g; Fat 40 g; Carbohydrate 30 g; Dietary Fibre 3 g; Cholesterol 115 mg; 2580 kJ (615 cal)

Place the tomatoes on a baking tray and drizzle with oil, vinegar and salt.

Let the roasted garlic cloves cool, then squeeze or peel them from their skins.

Place a sheet of pastry over each end of the tin, so they overlap in the middle.

RED CAPSICUM, TOMATO AND ONION TART

Preparation time: 35 minutes
+ 20 minutes refrigeration
Total cooking time: 1 hour 10 minutes
Serves 6

1 cup (125 g/4 oz) plain flour
1/2 cup (75 g/3 1/2 oz) wholemeal
    plain flour
100 g (3 1/2 oz) cold butter,
    chopped
1 tablespoon sesame seeds
1 egg, lightly beaten

Filling
500 g (1 lb) tomatoes, finely
    chopped
2 tablespoons tomato paste
1 teaspoon dried oregano
1/2 teaspoon sugar
1 tablespoon olive oil
3 red onions, sliced
1 teaspoon chopped thyme
3 red capsicums
1/3 cup (35 g/1 1/4 oz) finely
    grated Parmesan

1 Process the flours, butter and sesame seeds for about 15 seconds, or until the mixture resembles fine breadcrumbs. Add the egg and process in short bursts until the mixture just comes together. Add a little cold water if necessary. Turn out onto a lightly floured surface and quickly gather into a ball. Cover the pastry with plastic wrap and refrigerate for at least 20 minutes. Preheat the oven to moderately hot 200°C (400°F/ Gas 6) and grease a shallow 19 x 28 cm (7 1/2 x 11 inch) loose-based fluted flan tin.
2 Roll out the pastry on a sheet of baking paper until it is large enough to line the prepared tin. Lift the pastry into the tin, pressing well into the sides. Trim the edges with a sharp knife or by rolling a rolling pin across the top of the tin. Prick the pastry all over with a fork and bake for 12 minutes, or until just brown and dry. Allow to cool.
3 Heat the tomatoes, tomato paste, oregano and sugar in a pan. Bring to the boil, then reduce the heat and simmer for 15–20 minutes, or until thick. Allow to cool. Season to taste with salt and freshly ground black pepper.
4 Heat the oil in a pan and add the onion and thyme. Cook until the onion is soft and transparent.
5 Quarter the capsicums and remove the seeds and membrane. Grill, skin-side-up, until the skins have blistered. Cool in a plastic bag. Remove the skins and cut into quarters.
6 Spread the onion evenly over the base of the pastry shell and top with the tomato sauce. Sprinkle with cheese then top with the capsicum. Bake for 30 minutes, or until heated through and the pastry is crisp. Serve hot.

NUTRITION PER SERVE
Protein 10 g; Fat 20 g; Carbohydrate 30 g; Dietary Fibre 5 g; Cholesterol 80 mg; 1485 kJ (355 cal)

C O O K ' S F I L E

Variation: Yellow and green capsicums can also be used in this recipe.
Note: The pastry can be made ahead and kept stored in the freezer for up to 3 months; or in the refrigerator for up to 24 hours. Make sure it is well covered. Allow enough time to bring the pastry to room temperature before rolling it out.

Slice the red onions using a large, sharp cook's knife.

Place the flours, butter and sesame seeds in a food processor.

Lift the pastry into the prepared tin and press it well into the sides.

Heat the tomatoes, tomato paste, oregano and sugar in a pan.

Remove the blistered skin from the capsicums and cut them into pieces.

Spread the onions over the pastry shell and top with the tomato sauce.

FRIED GREEN TOMATO TART

Preparation time: 35 minutes
+ 15 minutes refrigeration
Total cooking time: 30 minutes
Serves 6

4 green tomatoes
1 tablespoon olive oil
20 g (3/4 oz) butter
1 teaspoon ground cumin
2 cloves garlic, crushed
1 sheet ready-rolled puff pastry
1/4 cup (60 ml/2 fl oz) sour cream
1 tablespoon chopped basil
2 tablespoons chopped parsley
1/2 cup (60 g/2 oz) grated
  Cheddar

1 Cut the tomatoes into thin slices. Heat the oil and butter in a frying pan and fry the cumin and garlic for 1 minute. Fry the tomatoes in batches for 2–3 minutes, until slightly softened. Drain on paper towels.

2 Cut a 24 cm (9½ inch) round from the puff pastry and place on a greased baking tray. Make a 2 cm (3/4 inch) border by scoring gently around the edge. Make small cuts inside the border. Refrigerate for 15 minutes. Preheat the oven to moderately hot 200°C (400°F/Gas 6) and bake for 10–15 minutes.

3 Combine the sour cream, basil and 1 tablespoon of parsley. Sprinkle the cheese over the centre of the pastry. Arrange 1 layer of tomatoes around the inside edge of the border and add the rest. Bake for 10 minutes. Place the cream mixture in the middle and add the remaining chopped parsley.

NUTRITION PER SERVE
Protein 5 g; Fat 20 g; Carbohydrate 10 g; Dietary Fibre 2 g; Cholesterol 40 mg; 1025 kJ (245 cal)

Lightly fry the tomatoes in batches until slightly softened.

Using the tip of a knife, make small cuts in the area inside the border.

Arrange the tomatoes around the inside edge of the border.

ASPARAGUS AND CRISPY PROSCIUTTO TARTS

Preparation time: 40 minutes
Total cooking time: 40 minutes
Serves 8

32 fresh asparagus spears
30 g (1 oz) butter
1 leek, sliced
8 slices prosciutto
2 sheets ready-rolled puff
    pastry
4 teaspoons wholegrain mustard
shaved Parmesan
1 egg, lightly beaten, to glaze

1 Preheat the oven to moderately hot 200°C (400°F/Gas 6). Break the woody ends from the asparagus. Melt 20 g (3/4 oz) of butter in a large heavy-based frying pan, add the leek and cook over low heat until soft. Remove from the pan and set aside. Melt the remaining butter in the pan, add the asparagus and toss gently over low heat for 1 minute. Drain on a paper towel.
2 Bake the prosciutto for 10 minutes, or until crispy. Allow to cool, then break into pieces and set aside.
3 Cut the pastry sheets into quarters. Spread the centre of each with 1/2 teaspoon of mustard. Divide the leek between the pastry sheets and top with 4 pieces of asparagus. Lay the prosciutto and Parmesan on top.
4 Fold 2 side corners up to meet and overlap, sealing with some beaten egg. Lay on a greased baking tray. Brush with the remaining beaten egg and bake for 25 minutes, or until golden.

NUTRITION PER SERVE
Protein 10 g; Fat 15 g; Carbohydrate 15 g; Dietary Fibre 2 g; Cholesterol 60 mg; 1035 kJ (245 cal)

Remove the woody ends from the asparagus.

When it is cool, break the prosciutto into pieces.

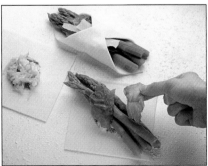

Top the asparagus with pieces of prosciutto.

FRENCH SHALLOT TATIN

Preparation time: 45 minutes
+ 20 minutes refrigeration
Total cooking time: 1 hour
Serves 4–6

750 g (1¹/₂ lb) French shallots
50 g (1³/₄ oz) butter
2 tablespoons olive oil
¹/₃ cup (60 g/2 oz) soft brown
   sugar
3 tablespoons balsamic vinegar

1 cup (125 g/4 oz) plain flour
60g (2 oz) cold butter, chopped
2 teaspoons wholegrain mustard
1 egg yolk

1 Peel the shallots, leaving the bases intact and tips exposed (see Hint).
2 Heat the butter and olive oil in a large pan. Cook the shallots for 15 minutes over low heat, then remove. Add the sugar, vinegar and 3 tablespoons of water to the pan and stir to dissolve the sugar. Add the shallots and simmer over low heat for 15–20 minutes, turning occasionally.
3 Preheat the oven to moderately hot 200°C (400°F/Gas 6). To make the pastry, process the flour and butter until crumbly. Add the mustard, egg yolk and 1 tablespoon of water. Process in short bursts until the mixture comes together. Add a little extra water if necessary. Turn the mixture out onto a floured surface and quickly gather into a ball. Cover with plastic wrap and refrigerate for 20 minutes.
4 Grease a shallow 20 cm (8 inch) round sandwich tin. Pack the shallots tightly into the tin and pour over any

syrup from the pan. Roll out the pastry on a sheet of baking paper to a circle, 1 cm (¹/₂ inch) larger than the tin. Lift the pastry into the tin and lightly push it down so it is slightly moulded over the shallots. Bake for 20–25 minutes, or until golden brown. Cool for 5 minutes on a wire rack. Place a serving dish over the tin and turn the tart out.

NUTRITION PER SERVE (6)
Protein 5 g; Fat 25 g; Carbohydrate 25 g; Dietary Fibre 2 g; Cholesterol 75 mg; 1360 kJ (325 cal)

COOK'S FILE

Hint: Put the unpeeled shallots in a bowl and cover with boiling water for 30 seconds. Drain and cool. This will make them easier to peel.

Return the shallots to the brown sugar and balsamic vinegar mixture in the pan.

Arrange the shallots over the base of the tin so that they are tightly packed.

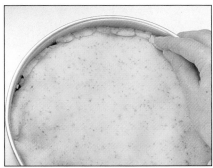
Lightly push the edges of the pastry down so that it lightly moulds over the shallots.

Cool the stock before adding the egg and Parmesan to prevent the egg scrambling.

Using a spoon, press the rice mixture into the base and sides of the flan tins.

ROAST CAPSICUM RICE TARTS

Preparation time: 45 minutes
Total cooking time: 1 hour 15 minutes
Serves 6

20 g (³/4 oz) butter
1/2 cup (95 g/3 oz) wild rice
1 cup (185 g/6 oz) short-grain brown rice
4 cups (1 litre) vegetable stock
2 eggs, beaten
1/2 cup (50 g/1³/4 oz) grated Parmesan
2 green capsicums
2 red capsicums
2 yellow capsicums
150 g (5 oz) Camembert cheese, thinly sliced
2 tablespoons oregano leaves

1 Melt the butter in a large pan, add the rice and stir, over low heat, until the rice is well coated. In a separate pan, heat the stock. Add 1/2 cup (125 ml/4 fl oz) of stock to the rice, stirring well. Increase the heat to medium and add the remaining stock 1 cup (250 ml/8 fl oz) at a time, stirring, until it has been absorbed. This will take about 30–40 minutes. Remove from the heat and cool. Add the eggs and Parmesan and season to taste with salt and black pepper.

2 Grease 6 loose-based fluted flan tins measuring 10 cm (4 inches) across the base. Divide the rice mixture between the tins and press it around the base and sides. Allow to cool completely.

3 Cut the capsicums into large flat pieces and grill, skin-side-up, until the skins have blackened and blistered. Cool in a plastic bag, remove the skins and slice.

4 Preheat the oven to moderately hot 200°C (400°F/Gas 6). Place the Camembert slices in the bottom of the lined tins and divide the capsicum evenly between the tarts. Bake for 30 minutes. Sprinkle the oregano leaves over the top and serve hot.

Remove the seeds and membrane and cut the capsicums into large flat pieces.

Divide the slices of Camembert between the lined flan tins.

NUTRITION PER SERVE
Protein 15 g; Fat 15 g; Carbohydrate 40 g; Dietary Fibre 3 g; Cholesterol 100 mg; 1515 kJ (360 cal)

PESTO AND ANCHOVY TART

Preparation time: 35 minutes
Total cooking time: 25–30 minutes
Serves 6

Pesto
1¹/2 cups (75 g/2¹/2 oz) basil
    leaves, firmly packed
2 cloves garlic
¹/2 cup (50 g/1³/4 oz) finely
    grated Parmesan
¹/2 cup (80 g/2³/4 oz) pine nuts,
    toasted
¹/4 cup (60 ml/2 fl oz) olive oil

375 g (12 oz) block puff pastry
1 egg yolk, lightly beaten
45 g (1¹/2 oz) can anchovies,
    drained
¹/3 cup (50 g/1³/4 oz) grated
    mozzarella cheese
¹/3 cup (35 g/1¹/4 oz) grated
    Parmesan

1 Place the basil, garlic, Parmesan and pinenuts in a food processor and chop finely. With the motor running, add the oil and process until well combined.
2 Preheat the oven to moderately hot 200°C (400°F/Gas 6). Roll the pastry into a rectangle 18 x 35 cm (7 x 14 inches), and 5 mm (¹/4 inch) thick. Cut a 2 cm (³/4 inch) strip from all the way round the edge of the pastry. Combine the lightly beaten egg yolk with 1 teaspoon of water. Use this to brush the edge of the pastry. Trim the pastry strips to fit around the rectangle and attach them to form a crust. Place on a lightly floured baking tray and, using the tip of a sharp knife, make small cuts all over

the base. Bake for 15 minutes. Press the centre of the pastry down with the back of a spoon and bake for a further 5 minutes, or until lightly golden. Allow to cool.
3 Spread the pesto mixture evenly over the base of the pastry. Cut the anchovies into thin strips and arrange

them over the top of the pesto. Sprinkle the grated mozzarella and Parmesan over the top and bake for 10 minutes, or until golden.

NUTRITION PER SERVE
Protein 15 g; Fat 40 g; Carbohydrate 25 g; Dietary Fibre 2 g; Cholesterol 70 mg; 2155 kJ (515 cal)

Add the olive oil to the chopped basil, garlic, Parmesan and pine nuts.

Attach the strips of pastry around the edge of the rectangle to make a crust.

Spread the pesto evenly over the base of the pastry.

INDEX

INTERNATIONAL GLOSSARY OF INGREDIENTS

baby squash	pattypan squash	cream	single/light whipping cream	self-raising flour	self-rising flour
besan flour	chickpea flour			semi-dried	sun-blushed
bocconcini	fresh baby mozzarella	eggplant	aubergine	smoked salmon	lox
broad beans	fava beans	flat-leaf parsley	Italian parsley	snow pea	mangetout
butternut pumpkin	squash	mince	ground meat	soft brown sugar	light brown sugar
		plain flour	all-purpose flour	spring onion	scallion
capsicum	pepper	polenta	cornmeal	thick cream	double/heavy cream
caster sugar	superfine sugar	prawn	shrimp	tomato paste (Aus./US)	tomato purée (UK)
coriander	cilantro	rocket	arugula		
cornflour	cornstarch	Roma tomato	plum/egg tomato	zucchini	courgette

This edition published in 2003 by Bay Books, an imprint of Murdoch Magazines Pty Limited, GPO Box 1203, Sydney NSW 2001, Australia.

Managing Editor: Rachel Carter **Designer:** Jacqueline Richards **Food Editor:** Roslyn Anderson **Editors:** Pip Vice, Elizabeth Cotton, Alison Moss **Recipe Development:** Roslyn Anderson, Amanda Cooper, Michelle Earl, Michelle Lawton, Stephanie Souvlis, Dimitra Stais, Alison Turner **Home Economists:** Anna Beaumont, Michelle Earl, Jo Glynn, Michelle Lawton, Kerrie Mullins, Angela Nahas, Kerrie Ray, Alison Turner **Photographers:** Andrew Elton, Ian Hofstetter (cover), Reg Morrison (steps) **Food Stylists:** Vicki Liley, Rosemary Mellish, Michelle Noerianto (cover) **Food Preparation:** Michelle Earl, Jo Forrest, Valli Little (cover).
Chief Executive: Juliet Rogers. **Publisher:** Kay Scarlett.

The nutritional information provided for each recipe does not include any accompaniments, such as rice, unless they are listed in the ingredients. The values are approximations and can be affected by biological and seasonal variations in food, the unknown composition of some manufactured foods and uncertainty in the dietary database. Nutrient data given are derived primarily from the NUTTAB95 database produced by the Australian New Zealand Food Authority.

ISBN 0 86411 598 9.
Printed by Sing Cheong Printing Co. Ltd. PRINTED IN CHINA